National Association for Girls & Women in Sport

RECE
DRAKE MEMOR

DEC 29 1983

STATE UNIVERSITY COLLEGE
BROCKPORT, N. Y. 14420

D1078413

Track and Field

NOVEMBER 1983-NOVEMBER 1985

Rules Chair
CLAUDIA BLACKMAN
Dept. of Physical Education,
Southern Illinois University,
Carbondale, Illinois

American Alliance for
Health, Physical Education,
Recreation and Dance

Copyright © 1983

American Alliance for
Health, Physical Education,
Recreation and Dance
1900 Association Drive
Reston, Virginia 22091

ISBN 0-88314-274-0

Purposes of the American Alliance For Health, Physical Education, Recreation and Dance

The American Alliance is an educational organization, structured for the purposes of supporting, encouraging, and providing assistance to member groups and their personnel throughout the nation as they seek to initiate, develop, and conduct programs in health, leisure, and movement-related activities for the enrichment of human life.

Alliance objectives include:

1. Professional growth and development—to support, encourage, and provide guidance in the development and conduct of programs in health, leisure, and movement-related activities which are based on the needs, interests, and inherent capacities of the individual in today's society.

2. Communication—to facilitate public and professional understanding and appreciation of the importance and value of health, leisure, and movement-related activities as they contribute toward human well-being.

3. Research—to encourage and facilitate research which will enrich the depth and scope of health, leisure, and movement-related activities; and to disseminate the findings to the profession and other interested and concerned publics.

4. Standards and guidelines—to further the continuous development and evaluation of standards within the profession for personnel and programs in health, leisure, and movement-related activities.

5. Public affairs—to coordinate and administer a planned program of professional, public, and governmental relations that will improve education in areas of health, leisure, and movement-related activities.

6. To conduct such other activities as shall be approved by the Board of Governors and the Alliance Assembly, provided that the Alliance shall not engage in any activity which would be inconsistent with the status of an educational and charitable organization as defined in Section 501 (c) (3) of the Internal Revenue Code of 1954 or any successor provision thereto, and none of the said purposes shall at any time be deemed or construed to be purposes other than the public benefit purposes and objectives consistent with such educational and charitable status.

Bylaws, Article III

New Publications

TIPS ON TRAINING

A new resource to provide coaches and athletic training personnel with an inside look at injury prevention and care.

NAGWS Special Publications

TIPS ON TRAINING
ADMINISTRATION OF GYMNASTICS MEETS: A HANDBOOK
    FOR TEACHERS AND COACHES
THE WONDER OF MOTION
EQUALITY IN SPORT FOR WOMEN
MOTIVATION IN COACHING A TEAM SPORT
NAGWS RESEARCH REPORTS
BLACK WOMEN IN SPORT

Contents

Foreword

NAGWS is proud to continue its publication of sport guides. On behalf of the Board of Directors I thank you for your time and expertise in writing and preparing the materials presented. As an association of volunteers we are appreciative of your part and present efforts and encourage you to encourage others to contribute. As programs for girls and women expand in scope and in number, the need for women in the sport field to serve as role models and experts becomes even more critical. Please let us know of your suggestions for improving and/or expanding NAGWS publications. You *are* NAGWS and *we* are here to serve you!

Bonnie Slatton
NAGWS President

Carol Bamberry
*NAGWS Guide
Coordinator*

The 80s appears to be a decade of active involvement in sport activity. The demand for current information by those involved in these activities has become epidemic. Avid participants, coaches, and teachers continue to look for the secrets of success in their sport activities. NAGWS continues to provide this information. Volunteer contributors provide information that can be used by players, coaches, teachers, and officials from all levels from elementary to high school, to college, and on the recreational level. As participation continues to increase across the country, we hope that you find the information contained herein helpful to you. Should you have valuable information that would be of use to others, we at NAGWS would be grateful to review it for use. The goal of NAGWS is to be "Committed to Quality and Equality;" we welcome your input in attaining this goal.

National Association for Girls & Women in Sport

The National Association for Girls and Women in Sport is a nonprofit, educational organization designed to serve the needs of participants, teachers, coaches, leaders, and administrators in sports programs for girls and women. It is one of seven associations of the American Alliance for Health, Physical Education, Recreation and Dance.

Purpose

The purpose of the National Association for Girls and Women in Sport is to foster the development of sports programs for the enrichment of the life of the participant.

Beliefs

The National Association for Girls and Women in Sport believes that:
Sports are an integral part of the culture in which we live.

Sports programs are a part of the total educational experience of the participant when conducted in educational institutions.

Opportunities for instruction and participation in sports appropriate to her skill level should be included in the experience of every girl.

Sports skills and sports participation are valuable social and recreational tools which may be used to enrich the lives of women in our society.

Competition and cooperation may be demonstrated in all sports programs, although the type and intensity of the competition and cooperation will vary with the degree or level of skill of the participants.

An understanding of the relationship between competition and cooperation and the utilization of both within the accepted framework of our society is one of the desirable outcomes of sports participation.

Physical activity is important in the maintenance of the general health of the participant.

Participation in sports contributes to the development of self-confidence and to the establishment of desirable interpersonal relationships.

Functions

The National Association for Girls and Women in Sport promotes desirable sports programs through:
Formulating and publicizing guiding principles and standards for the

administrator, leader, official, and player.

Publishing and interpreting rules governing sports for girls and women.

Providing the means for training, evaluating, and rating officials.

Disseminating information on the conduct of girls' and women's sports.

Stimulating, evaluating, and disseminating research in the field of girls' and women's sports.

Cooperating with allied groups interested in girls' and women's sports in order to formulate policies and rules that affect the conduct of women's sports.

Providing opportunities for the development of leadership among girls and women for the conduct of their sports programs.

Standards in Sports for Girls & Women

Standards in sports activities for girls and women should be based upon the following:

Sports activities for girls and women should be taught, coached, and officiated by qualified women whenever possible.

Programs should provide every girl with a wide variety of activities.

The results of competition should be judged in terms of *benefits to the participants* rather than by winning championships or the athletic or by commercial advantage to schools or organizations.

Health and Safety Standards for Players

Careful supervision of the health of all players must be provided by:
1. An examination by a qualified physician
2. Written permission by a qualified physician after serious illness or injury
3. Removal of players when they are injured, overfatigued, or show signs of emotional instability
4. A healthful, safe, and sanitary environment for sports activity
5. Limitation of competition to a geographical area which will permit players to return at reasonable hours; provision for safe transportation

General Policies

Arrange matches between teams of comparable ability and maturity.

Schedule games and practices so as not to place demands on teams or players which would jeopardize the educational objectives of the comprehensive sports program.

Discourage girls from practicing or playing with more than one team during a sport season.

Promote social events with all forms of competition.

Sources of Information & Service

All requests for information about services should be addressed to: Executive Director, National Association for Girls and Women in Sport (NAGWS), AAHPERD, 1900 Association Drive, Reston, VA, 22091.

Coaches Academies of the Affiliated National Coaches Council

The National Coaches Academies were formed by the NAGWS to:

(1) provide a channel of direct communication among coaches at all educational levels

(2) assist in the formulation dissemination of guiding principles, standards, and policies for conducting competitive sports programs for girls and women

(3) keep members informed of current coaching techniques and trends

(4) sponsor clinics and conferences in sports and coaching skills

(5) provide opportunities for members to become appointed representatives to the National Governing Body of a particular sport, and/or sports-specific rules committees

(6) promote cooperative efforts with other sports-centered organizations

(7) endorse international exchange programs

(8) provide a united body for positive political action in the realm of girls' and women's athletics.

Academies for 11 sports have been established. (Note the application blank for specific listings.) Membership in each Academy is open to any coach of girls' or women's sports or any interested person.

Get involved . . . Join NOW.

Direct questions to:

Veronica Harris, Chair
National Coaches Council
127 West 104th Place
Chicago, IL 60629

OR

Carol L. Thompson
NAGWS Executive Director
1900 Association Dr.
Reston, VA 22091
(703) 476-3450

Sports Academies of the Affiliated National Coaches Council

National Association for Girls & Women in Sport: AAHPERD
1900 Association Dr., Reston, VA 22091

FOR OFFICE USE:
DT: _____ AMT: _____
CK: _____

NAME _____ _____ _____
       last   first   initial

ADDRESS _____
         street

_____ _____ _____
    city   state   zip

AAHPERD MEMBERS: Membership number as it appears on your journal label: _____

Teaching/Coaching level (please check): _____ College _____ Jr. College _____ High School
_____ Jr. High _____ Elementary _____ Other

Please check the academies you wish to join:*
☐ Badminton ☐ Basketball ☐ Field Hockey
☐ Gymnastics ☐ Softball ☐ Swimming/Diving ☐ Synchronized Swimming ☐ Tennis
☐ Track & Field ☐ Volleyball ☐ Soccer

I am willing to serve on an Academy committee: ☐

*AAHPERD members: $10.00 for one Academy and $2.00 for each additional Academy. Non-AAHPERD members $20.00 for one Academy and $2.00 each additional Academy. ($10.00 non-membership fee may be applied at any time toward AAHPERD membership.)

Please send AAHPERD membership information: _____ yes _____ no

NAGWS Sports Guides Committees Interest Indicator

The NAGWS Sport Guide Committee is endeavoring to broaden its base of personnel and to strengthen services to *Guide* readers. The purpose of this form is to offer readers an opportunity to join us in meeting this need. Please complete this form and send it to NAGWS, 1900 Association Dr., Reston, VA 22091.

Name _____

Professional Address _____

City _____ State _____ Zip Code _____

1. Check the Sport Committee(s) which would be of interest to you:

___ Aquatics	___ Fencing	___ Soccer
___ Archery	___ Field Hockey	___ Softball
___ Badminton	___ Flag Football	___ Speedball
___ Basketball	___ Golf	___ Squash
___ Bowling	___ Gymnastics	___ Synchronized Swimming
___ Competitive Swimming	___ Lacrosse	___ Team Handball
___ Cross-country Track	___ Orienteering	___ Tennis
___ Cross-country Skiing	___ Racquetball	___ Track and Field
___ Diving	___ Skiing	___ Volleyball
		___ Water Polo

2. Would you like to serve as a member of a Sports Guide Committee of your interest?   ___ Yes   ___ No

3. Would you consider submitting an article to a Guide Committee as a prospective author?   ___ Yes   ___ No
    Possible topic or title _____

4. Can you suggest topics for articles which you would like to have included in future *Guides*? (Please indicate sport.) _____
    _____

5. Are there others whom you would recommend for consideration as possible committee members or authors? Please indicate below. (Use additional paper, if necessary.)

    Name _____ Sport(s) _____

    Professional Address _____

    City _____ State _____ Zip Code _____
    Sports Committee Member ☐   Prospective Author ☐ (check one)

NAGWS
Official Track and Field Rules

NAGWS Track and Field Rules Committee*
1983-84

CLAUDIA BLACKMAN, *Chair,* Dept. of Physical Education, Southern Illinois University, Carbondale, IL 62901 (1981-85)

NELL JACKSON, *Rules Interpreter,* West Gymnasium, State University of New York, Binghamton, NY 13901 (1981-85)

LURLINE JONES, *PTO Chair,* 940 E. McPherson St., Philadelphia, PA 19150

---

*The 1983-84 Committee prepared the material in this *Guide.*

Summary of Major Rules Changes

Rule 1.

A note has been added informing readers that the 1983-85 *Guide* will be the last edition to include both yard and meter distances. Beginning with the 1985-87 *Guide* only meter distances will appear.

SECTION 3 (Rule 8, Section 5).
The order of events of the heptathalon has been changed to 100 meter hurdles, high jump, shotput, 200 meters, long jump, javelin, and 800 meter.

Rule 5.

SECTION 3g.
Starting blocks should be used in races or relays when that race or relay leg does not exceed 400 meters. When starting blocks are unavailable a crouching position must be assumed on the start.

SECTION 6b(3).
After the qualifying round, relay teams will be allowed two substitutes due to injury or illness (with a doctor's certification).

SECTION 6b(5).
At the time of the declaration of entries, the declarer must indicate whether relay teams entered are to compete but designation of the make-up of a relay team need not be made until a designated time before the start of the first round of the event as determined by the meet director or by the rules.

Rule 6.

SECTION 3a(5).
Beginning in November 1985 a new rule excluding the use of the triangular crossbar will go into effect.

SECTION 3b(1).
Until there is one competitor remaining or there is a tie, the bar should never be raised by less than 2 centimeters after each round. In combined events the raising shall be uniformly 3 centimeters throughout the competition.

SECTION 6b.

A competitor in a field event shall be disqualified if she uses an implement or equipment that has been illegally altered after having been officially inspected or if she uses an unapproved or illegal implement or equipment. All records, performances or points scored with the use of such implement or equipment shall be declared null and void.

Rule 8.

SECTION 6d.

The sentence "one system of timing" shall be used throughout the competition.

SECTION 6m.

The starting height for the high jump shall be determined by the competition. The bar shall be raised at 3 centimeter (1⅛ ") increments. Competitors may begin jumping at any height and may jump at their discretion at any sequence.

Rule 10.

SECTION 2e.

Records may be set on tracks with more than 8 lanes as long as the radius of the outside lane does not exceed 60 meters.

Practice and Techniques of Officiating Section

SECTION VI. 6k.

The chief timekeeper shall confer with the track referee when a time of "no-time" is recorded.

SECTION VII. 1p.

When, during the warmup period, the opening height proves to be too stringent for all competitors this should be reported to the meet director who should take appropriate action by lowering the opening height.

SECTION VIII. 12d.

The chute inspector shall designate a substitute for a competitor unable to exit the chute.

SECTION IX. 5.

Where feasible a combined-events coordinator should be appointed to see that the events proceed expeditiously.

Contents for Official Rules

Official Track and Field Rules for Girls and Women

Note: Rules which have been reworded or clarified are designated by a check (√). Changes and/or additions in rules have been indicated by underlining.

Rule 1. Events

SECTION 1. Outdoor Track Events

Track events at all official outdoor track meets for girls and women may include any of the following:

Ages 9-10-11

RUNNING

English	*Metric*
50 yard dash*	50 meter dash
75 yard dash	70 meter dash
100 yard dash	100 meter dash
220 yard dash	200 meter dash
440 yard dash	400 meter dash
880 yard run	800 meter run
Race Walking	Race Walking

RELAYS

220 yard (4 × 55)	200 meter (4 × 50)
220 yd shuttle (4 × 55)	200 m shuttle (4 × 50)
440 yard (4 × 110)	400 meter (4 × 100)

HURDLES

50 yard (30″)	50 meter (76 cm)

Ages 12-13-14

RUNNING

English	*Metric*
50 or 60 yard dash	50 meter dash
100 yard dash	100 meter dash
220 yard dash	200 meter dash
440 yard dash	400 meter dash
English	*Metric*
880 yard run	800 meter run

*The 1983-85 *Guide* will be the last edition to include both yard and meter distances. Beginning with the 1985-87 *Guide* only meter distances will appear.

English	*Metric*
Mile run	1500 meter run
Two mile run	3000 meter run
Race Walking	Race Walking

RELAYS

220 yard (4 × 55)	200 meter (4 × 50)
440 yard (4 × 110)	400 meter (4 × 100)
880 yard (4 × 220)	800 meter (4 × 200)
880 yard Medley	800 meter Medley
(110-110-220-440)	(100-100-200-400)
Mile (4 × 440)	1600 meter (4 × 400)

HURDLES

50 yard (30″)	50 meter (76 cm.)
80 yard (30″)	80 meter (76 cm.)
110 yard (30″)	**100 meter (76 cm.)**

Ages 15 and over

RUNNING

50 or 60 yard dash	50 or 60 meter dash
100 yard dash	100 meter dash
220 yard dash	200 meter dash
440 yard dash	400 meter dash
880 yard run	800 meter run
Mile run	1500 meter run
Two mile run	3000 meter run
Three mile run	5000 meter run
Race Walking	Race Walking

RELAYS

440 yard (4 × 110)	400 meter (4 × 100)
880 yard (4 × 220)	800 meter (4 × 200)
880 yard Medley	800 meter Medley
(110-110-220-440)	(100-100-200-400)
Mile (4 × 440)	1600 meter (4 × 400)
Two mile (4 × 880)	3200 meter (4 × 800)

English	*Metric*
HURDLES	
50 yard (30″)	50 meter (76 cm.)
80 yard (30″)	80 meter (76 cm.)
110 yard (30″ or 33″)	100 meter (76 cm. or 84 cm.)
220 yard (30″)	200 meter (76 cm.)
330 yard (30″)	300 meter (76 cm.)
	400 meter (76 cm.)

College and Open

RUNNING	
100 yard dash	100 meter dash
220 yard dash	200 meter dash
440 yard dash	400 meter dash
880 yard run	800 meter run
Mile run	1500 meter run
Two mile run	3000 meter run
Three mile run	5000 meter run
Six mile run	10,000 meter run
Race Walking	Race Walking

RELAYS	
440 yard (4 × 110)	400 meter (4 × 100)
880 yard (4 × 220)	800 meter (4 × 200)
880 yard Medley	800 meter Medley
(110-110-220-440)	(100-100-200-400)
Mile (4 × 440)	1600 meter (4 × 400)
Two mile (4 × 880)	3200 meter (4 × 800)

HURDLES	
	100 meter (33″ or 84 cm.)
	400 meter (30″ or 76 cm.)

SECTION 2. Outdoor Field Events

Field events at all official outdoor track and field meets for girls and women may include any of the following:

Ages 9-10-11	*Ages 12-13-14*	*Ages 15 & Over*
Shot Put (6 lbs.)	Shot Put (8 lbs.)	Shot Put (8 lbs.* or 4 kilo-8lbs., 13 oz.)
Softball Throw	Softball Throw	Discus
Standing Long Jump	Standing Long Jump	Javelin
Running Long Jump	Running Long Jump	Running Long Jump
High Jump	High Jump	High Jump
	Discus	
	Javelin	

College & Open
Shot Put (4 kilo — 8 lbs., 13 oz.)   Long Jump
Discus   High Jump
Javelin

SECTION 3. Outdoor Combined Events (12 and over)

Pentathlon (100 meter hurdles, shotput, high jump, long jump, 800 meter run)

Heptathalon (100 meter hurdles, high jump, shotput, 200 meters, long jump, javelin, 800 meter)

SECTION 4. Indoor Track Events

Track events at all official indoor meets for girls and women may include any of the following:

English	*Metric*
50 or 60 yard dash	50 or 60 meter dash
50 or 60 yard hurdles	50 or 60 meter hurdles
70 yard hurdles	
220 yard dash	200 meter dash
300 yard dash	300 meter dash
440 yard dash	400 meter dash
600 yard dash	600 meter dash

---

*This will be the final year that an 8 lb. shot may be used.

880 yard run	800 meter run
*1000 yard run	*1000 meter run
*Mile run	*1500 meter run
*Two mile run	*300 meter run
**3 mile run	**5000 meter run
4 lap relay (4 × 1 lap)	4 lap relay (4 × 1 lap)
*Mile relay (4 × 440)	*1600 meter relay (4 × 400)
*Two mile relay (4 × 880)	*3200 meter relay (4 × 800)
*Distance medley relay (880, 440, 1320, mile)	*Distance medley relay (800, 400, 1200, 1600)

SECTION 5. Indoor Field Events

High Jump   Long Jump   Shot Put

SECTION 6. Indoor Combined Events

Triathlon (50 or 60 meter hurdles, shot put, high jump)
Pentathlon (50 or 60 meter hurdles, shot put, high jump, long jump, 800 meter run)

Rule 2. Scoring

SECTION 1. Individual Events and Relays

a. In a track and field meet where the result of a competition is to be determined by the scoring of points, the method of scoring shall be as follows:

Number of Teams Competing	Individual Scoring	Relay Scoring
2	5-3-1	5
3	5-3-2-1	5-3
4	6-4-3-2-1	6-4-2
5	6-4-3-2-1	6-4-3-2
6	10-8-6-4-2-1	10-8-6-4-2
7 or more	10-8-6-4-2-1	10-8-6-4-2-1

*all ages except 9 through 11
**all ages except 9 through 14

b. In dual and triangular meets, only one relay team per school may score.
c. If the best performance of a competitor in a field event determined by distance is identical to another competitor's, the next best effort shall break the tie.
d. If there is a tie between two or more competitors for any place which receives a score in either a track or field event, the sum of the points of the places involved shall be divided equally between the tying competitors.
e. Points given for the various places are awarded to the competitor's team and totaled cumulatively during the meet.
f. The combined events competition (triathlon, pentathlon, heptathlon) shall be scored as an event provided it is held in conjunction with the regularly scheduled meet.

SECTION 2. Total Team Score*

a. The final score for a team at the conclusion of a meet will be the sum of all points awarded in accordance with the above section. The team receiving the highest number of points shall be declared the winner of the meet.
b. When two or more teams have the same number of points, the team scoring the most first places shall be declared the winner. If the tie still exists, the team scoring the most second places shall be the winner. This procedure will be continued for the ensuing places until the tie is broken, if possible.

Rule 3. Protests

1. Protests relating to matters which develop during the conduct of the program shall be made at once, if possible, but not later than 30 minutes after the result has been officially announced, or within 15 minutes in a preliminary round.
2. Any such protests must be made in writing by a responsible team representative and submitted to the meet referee.

---

*See the Cross-country and Combined Events Sections for their individual procedures.

3. A decision will be given by the Games Committee. In the absence of a games committee, the meet referee or the meet director will have the responsibility for the final decision.

✗ Rule 4. General Rules of Competition

1. A competitor may participate in age categories above that of the competitor but may not participate in those age categories below the age of the competitor.
2. All the events listed in any age group do not have to be included in any one meet.
3. The order of events shall not be changed nor the time period between events.
4. A competitor may participate in an unlimited number of events. However, in competition at levels other than intercollegiate, the state or local governing body may limit the number of events in which a competitor may compete.
5. If a competitor participates in any of the combined events competitions, the competitor may not compete in any individual or relay events on the same day.
6. After a deadline for confirmation has been set, or a scratch meeting held, a competitor must compete in the events entered or be barred from the remaining competition and the results of the previous events will be invalidated. If she is injured or becomes ill during the meet, a medical verification allows the completed events to be counted, but she will be barred from further competition.
7. Any competitor who refuses to obey the directions of the referee or any other official, or who acts in an unsporting manner shall be disqualified from any event by the referee(s) or Games Committee. (Unsporting conduct is conduct which is unfair, unethical, or dishonorable. It includes action and/or language which is a discredit to the individual or the individual's school. It also includes disrespectfully addressing an official, using profanity or throwing a baton following a relay.)

8. Competitors may compete in bare feet, unless prohibited by local or state law, with one shoe or with both shoes. The purpose of the shoe is to provide the competitor protection and stability. The shoe shall not be constructed to give additional assistance. The shoes of the competitors in events other than the long jump shall not have soles which exceed 13 millimeters (½") or a heel which exceeds the sole by more than 6 millimeters (¼"). The heels of the long jump shoes shall not exceed 25 millimeters (1") in total thickness including any heel inserts or pads which may be used.

   The number of spikes is limited to a maximum of six in the sole and two in the heel with the exception of the high jump and the javelin where a maximum of four spikes is permitted in the heel. (Provision may be made in the soles and heels for exchanging the position of the spikes provided that the maximum number allowed is not exceeded.)

   The spike length is to conform to the type of track surface as specified by the meet director. The dimensions of the spike projecting from the sole or the heel must not exceed 25 millimeters in length or four millimeters in diameter. When synthetic competitive surfaces are used, the length of the spike projecting from the sole or heel must not exceed nine millimeters with the exception of the high jump and the javelin where the length must not exceed 12 millimeters.

   The sole and/or heel may be constructed with grooves, ridges, indentations or protuberances provided these are of the same or similar material as the sole itself. Such ridges or protuberances are regarded as part of the sole, the total thickness of which must not exceed 13 millimeters.

9. Competitors must wear an official school uniform that is designed for competition and worn so as not to be objectionable. The clothing shall be non-transparent even when wet. Members of a relay team shall wear uniforms of a similar design and color(s). However, variations in *shorts style* among a team are permitted; the addition, by some team members, of t-shirts worn under shirts or tights worn under shorts is permissible as well.

10. All equipment and implements used in the competition shall be weighed, measured and approved by meet officials.

11. Numbers shall be worn by all competitors. Jumpers and combined events athletes may wear their numbers on either

the front or back of their blouses (when jumping). Runners competing in races of 100 meters (1000 yards) or greater shall wear numbers on the front of their blouses. All other competitors shall have their numbers securely fastened to the back of their blouses. Competitors not wearing their numbers during competition shall be disqualified. Competitors losing their numbers during the competition shall receive consideration by the Games Committee. Numbers may be required on both the front and back of the blouse. Additional numbers may be worn on the sides of the shorts to identify competitors when photoelectric equipment is used. Numbers shall be worn as designated by the Games Committee.

12. The athlete shall report at least 15 minutes (or within the time established by the meet director) before the event to the designated clerk. The announcer shall give proper announcements to aid the competitors in reporting on time to the clerk of the course or the field event judges.

13. A competitor with the permission of and accompanied by an official may leave the immediate area of the field event or combined events competition. Otherwise, the competitor shall be disqualified from further competition.

14. No competitor shall receive assistance from any other person (another competitor, teammate, fan, coach, or official) during the competition. Such occurrence shall bring a caution from the referee, field judge, etc., and any further repetition shall cause disqualification from that competition. (This does not mean that fans, teammates, and coaches will not be allowed to show encouragement to competing competitors.)

15. Athletes competing in both track and field events or in two or more field events simultaneously shall be allowed to take their trials in a different order from that arranged prior to the start of competition. Running events take precedence over field events. If a competitor is participating in a field event, and a running event is called, the competitor must leave the field event. An athlete who leaves the event to compete in a running event must be given 10 minutes recovery time from the completion of the running event before she must perform her next trial. In cases where an athlete is unable to take a practice run-through or throw prior to reporting for the running event (due to circumstances resulting from meet

management) she shall be given 2 run-throughs or throws as warm-ups amongst the ongoing competition.

16. In meets of 4 or more teams, a field event athlete is not allowed to have more than one trial recorded in a single round of competition. Trials missed in a prior round cannot be made up.

17. In dual or triangular meets, a field event athlete who must report to a running event may take more than one consecutive trial (not to exceed two) to replace said trials missed while running or performing the warmup attempts.

    Note: The high jump bar shall never be lowered. Athletes may take their warmup attempts at the height of the bar upon their return or a jump without the bar.

18. When a competitor in an individual event who has qualified in a preliminary trial withdraws from the competition in the semifinals or the finals, the competitor may not be replaced by a substitute.

19. No official record for an event may be claimed unless all official standards for that event have been met.

Rule 5. Running Events

SECTION 1. Outdoor Facilities—Track and Lanes, Equipment, Supplies

a. The track shall be a surveyed 400 meter or 440 yard course with minimal width lanes of 30 inches and a maximum of 48 inches.

b. The running track will be measured 8″ inside the lane with the exception of the curb lane which will be measured one foot (12″) inside the lane. (If there is no curb, the inside lane will also be measured 8″ inside the lane.) The width of the lane lines shall be 2″.

c. The maximum inclination permitted for the track shall not exceed 1:100 in a lateral direction and 1:1000 in the running direction.

d. The blocks must be constructed without springs or other devices which would provide artificial assistance. The blocks must be adjustable and must be placed and removed easily without damaging the track. Competitors may use their own blocks provided they meet the above specifications unless prohibited by the meet organizers.

SECTION 2. Determination of Heats and Lanes

a. Heats shall be held in all track events in which the number of competitors is too large to allow the competition to be conducted satisfactorily in a final.

 1. In races of up to and including 400 meters (440 yards), the number of competitors in heats and finals shall not exceed the number of lanes of the track.
 2. If more competitors are declared for the 800 meter (880 yard) run than the number of available lanes, trials shall be run. If trials are run, the number of finalists shall correspond to the number of lanes of the track.
 3. If more than 12 competitors are declared for the 1500 meter (one mile) run, trials shall be run. When trials are run, twelve (12) shall be selected for the finals. For one or two day meets with more than 12 competitors, sections may be run composed of competitors with comparable times.
 4. If more than 18 competitors are declared for the 3000 meter (2 mile) or 24 for the 5000 meter (3 mile) runs, trials shall be run. If trials are run, the number of finalists shall correspond to double the number of lanes of the track. In the best interest of all concerned, the Games Committee or meet director may schedule these races to be run in sections in lieu of trials if notification is provided in the original schedule. Sections shall be composed of competitors with comparable times.
 5. The 10,000 meter run shall be run as a final.
 6. In relay events up to and including the 1600 meters (4 × 400) or 1 mile (4 × 440 yards), the number of teams in heats and finals shall not exceed the number of lanes available.
 7. In one day meets, sections may be run as finals in events 400 meters or longer at the discretion of the meet director.

b. At least the first two and preferably the first three places in preliminary heats shall advance to the succeeding round. Other qualifiers may be decided according to their times. A minimum amount of time must be allowed between rounds of competition:

 45 minutes in events through 300 meters (330 yards);
 90 minutes in events 400 meters (440 yards) through 1000 meters (1,100 yards);
 3 hours in events of 1500 meters (1 mile) or more.

c. Heats for the preliminary and final rounds of the running events shall be formed under the direction of the Games Committee or the meet director. All confirmed entries for the preliminary rounds shall be assigned to heats in the order in which they are ranked by performance, working alternately from left to right and right to left (see PTO "Track Referee"). Exceptions are provided when two competitors from the same team fall in the same heat (in which case the slower competitor would be exchanged with someone of near equivalent place and time in an adjoining heat). Lanes will be assigned by draw for races on both the straightaway and the curve.

d. Competitors will be assigned to heats for the succeeding rounds and finals according to place finish rather than by times. When additional qualifiers are admitted on a time basis, this will be weighed secondly to the place of finish. The first place finishers are assigned to heats, then second place finishers, and so on. Again, the assignments are made from left to right, and right to left. If two competitors from the same team fall in the same heat, one of the competitors may be exchanged with a competitor in another heat if the placements and/or times are similar.

e. If there is a tie in any heat which affects qualifications for the next semifinals or finals, the tying competitors shall both qualify if lanes or positions are available. If they are not available, the tying competitors shall compete again for the available lane or position.

f. During succeeding rounds and finals, in all races both on the straightaway and around the curve, competitors will be assigned lanes by draw. In races of 1500 meters (1 mile) and longer, positions are assigned by draw.

g. If the preliminary round is substantially affected by a number of confirmed competitors failing to report, the heat may be redrawn for greater fairness to the competitors. If the number reporting falls below the number required for a preliminary round, the trial round may be eliminated in that event and the competitors advanced to the succeeding round.

h. For all relays and semifinals with 2 heats, the first two places plus the next four best times shall qualify for the finals. If 3 heats or semifinals are required, the first two places in each heat, plus the next two best times overall shall qualify for the finals.

SECTION 3. Conduct of Race

a. The direction of running around the turn shall be counterclockwise.

b. In races which include at least one turn, the starting line must be staggered by measurement for each lane to compensate for varying distances of those lanes around the curve.

c. All races up to and including the 400 meter shall be run in lanes with one runner to a lane. The 200 meter will be run from a one-turn stagger and the 400 meter from a two-turn stagger.

d. In all races run in lanes, the competitor should stay in the assigned lane from start to finish. Any runner deliberately running outside the lane shall be disqualified. A competitor who has unintentionally run outside the lane and who has not interfered with an opponent may not be disqualified at the discretion of the referee. If, however, significant advantage was derived from this action, intentional or not, disqualification shall result.

e. When running on a curve, a runner will be disqualified for taking three or more successive steps on or over the inside lane line with either or both feet.

f. In races of 1500 meters (1 mile) or longer a curved, involuted (waterfall) starting line will be used (see Appendix C).

√g. Starting blocks should be used in races of relays when that race or relay leg does not exceed 400 meters (440 yds). When starting blocks are unavailable a crouching position must be assumed on the start. Both feet and hands must be in contact with the ground when using starting blocks or when in a crouching position. Starting blocks will not be allowed for distances greater than 400 meters (440 yds).

h. The competitors shall not touch either the starting line or the ground in front of it with their hands or feet when on their marks or in the set position. *Note:* The baton may rest upon the track and ahead of the starting line.

i. The starting command of races through 400 meters (440 yards) will be "On your mark," "Set," and when all competitors are steady the gun shall be fired. For races over 400 meters (440 yards), the commands will be "Runners Set," and when all competitors are steady the gun shall be fired. A whistle technique can be used as an alternative. (See PTO "Starter.")

j. On the command "Set," all competitors will immediately move to their set positions. A runner who so fails to comply with this command within a reasonable time shall be charged with a false start.

k. A competitor leaving the mark before the gun is fired shall be charged with a false start. Any competitor making 2 false starts (or 3 in the case of the combined events) shall be disqualified from that particular event. A false start shall be called if a competitor leaves the mark with the hand or foot, and/or is in motion after the "Set" but before the shot is fired.

l. A competitor shall make an honest effort to qualify or place. Intentionally taking two false starts, not leaving the blocks after a legitimate start, jogging a dash run, or not attempting to run a race after reporting are examples of a lack of honest effort. If an honest effort is not made, the competitor shall be barred from all remaining competition in that meet and the results of the previous events will be invalidated.

m. When a one-turn staggered start is used, competitors may not break to the inside lane until the first turn is finished. In races in which a curved start is used, a competitor may break to the inside lane as soon as possible.

n. In races where breaking to the inside lane is permitted, a competitor may break to the inside lane when the progress of another competitor will not be impeded.

o. Competitors shall be recalled if a runner is jostled and falls or is placed at a distinct disadvantage while in the first turn of races not run in lanes, or as they move to the inside of the straightaway after running one turn in lanes as in the 800 meter (880 yard) run. See PTO "Starter."

p. Competitors shall be prepared to run their events in such a manner as to ensure their best effort and at the same time permit their competitors equal opportunities for fair competition. Competitors displaying unsporting conduct during the competition shall be disqualified. Examples of actions which shall result in disqualification follow:

- jostling, cutting across the path, or obstructing another competitor so as to impede progress. Direct contact is not necessary; any action that causes a competitor to break stride or lose momentum can lead to disqualification.
- veering to the right or left on the final straightaway or on the backstretch so as to impede a challenging runner and/or force the competitor to run a greater distance.
- forcing way between two leading competitors, making direct contact so as to impede the progress of either.
- running inside the curb, thereby gaining an advantage by improv-

ing position or shortening the course. (This does not pertain to a runner being temporarily forced off the inside of the track.)
- leaving the track voluntarily.
- holding the hands of a teammate during the race or at the finish.
- impeding the progress of a runner by deliberate "boxing" by two or more competitors. (However, it should be noted that unintentional "boxes" occur frequently during a race when a runner on the inside finds two or more opponents to the front and to the side. Care must be taken to determine between strategy on the one hand and unsporting impeding of fair progress on the other.)

q. If in any race a competitor is disqualified for interfering with another competitor, the referee shall have power to order the race to be rerun excluding the disqualified competitor. In the case of a heat, the referee may permit any competitors affected by the act resulting in disqualification (other than the disqualified competitor) to compete in the subsequent round. Obviously, such a decision must be made with discretion. Factors related to order of events, responsibilities of competitors in other events, the nature of the event (i.e., 100 meters, 5000 meters) must be considered if rerunning of a trial or final round is to be scheduled. Whenever possible, the advancement of the affected runner to the next round is preferred. Where races or relays are run in lanes which are already filled by qualifiers, two sections of a heat or final may be run if necessary.

r. In all races of 200 meters (220 yards) or less, information on wind velocity must be provided for record consideration. (See "PTO of Wind Gauge Operator" or "Records" for information on Anemometer regulations.)

s. Finish twine or tape shall be stretched across the track at the appropriate height (approximately chest high) between the finish posts immediately above the edge of the finish line nearest the start except when fully automatic timing devices are used. This may be discontinued if the wind direction or velocity might create confusion on the part of either officials or competitors.

t. A competitor shall be placed at the finish in the order in which any part of the torso (i.e., torso as distinguished from the head, neck, arms, legs, or feet) crosses the perpendicular plane of the nearest edge of the finish line.

u. If photoprints or phototiming devices are used, such prints shall be taken from a point on the finish line extended which adequately shows the finish of each competitor. These prints should take precedence in the placing and timing of track events. Fully automatic times of all races run distances of up through 10,000 meters or more shall be recorded in 1/100th of a second.

v. Hand times for all running events for races over 400 meters (440 yards) will be recorded in tenths of seconds. When converting a time from 1/100th to 1/10th of a second, it shall be rounded up to the next longer 1/10th of a second (e.g., 55.44 becomes 55.5).

w. Electronic Timing (fully automatic timing)
Electronically timed marks can only be submitted if fully automatic electrical timed equipment is used. This means the electrical timing device must be started by a contact on the Starter's pistol or any similar apparatus at the instant of the flash from the charge. The finishing times (hundredths) and the finishing places of the competitors shall be read from a photo-finished (moving film) picture. Electronic timing standards are arrived at by adding twenty-four one-hundredths second (.24) to the hand timed standards for all track events up to and including 220 yards. For races over 220 yards and through 440 yards, fourteen one-hundredths second (.14) is added.

SECTION 4. Middle Distance and Distance

a. In the 800 meter (880 yard) run, competitors shall run from a one-turn stagger and will break to the inside lane at the flag or pole at the beginning of the straightaway.

b. The curved line (involuted) or waterfall start shall be used for all distances 1500 meters and longer. Positions will be drawn so that competitors are arranged side-by-side behind the starting line. Competitors may be aligned in such a manner that as many as 12 to 18 may stand abreast upon an 8 or 9 lane track.* When drawing for positions, the first position is to the inside edge of the track and the highest position is toward the outside edge. At the gun, the competitors may break to the inside lane taking care not to foul.

c. In races of 800 meters or longer, an official shall give cumulative race times of each of the competitors as they pass the starting line. No other person may give this information to the competitors.

---

*If the number of competitors warrants, two rows of competitors should be assembled behind the curved starting line.

d. In races of 800 meters or longer, the final lap of the leading competitor shall be signalled by the ringing of a bell or the firing of a starting gun.

e. In races of 1500 meters or longer, each competitor shall be notified of the number of laps yet to be completed by a lap counter near the finish line.

f. Lapped runners should continue to run in the inside lane and should make every effort to run their best race.

SECTION 5. Hurdles

a. Equipment
   1. A hurdle shall be made of wood or metal, and shall consist of two bases and two uprights supporting a rectangular frame reinforced by one or more crossbars, the uprights being fixed at the extreme ends of the base. The hurdle may be adjustable in height, but shall be rigidly fastened at the required height for each event. The hurdle shall be designed so that (irrespective of its height) a force of at least 3.6 kilograms (8 lbs.) and not more than 4 kilograms (8 lbs., 13 oz.) applied to the center of the top edge of the (top) crossbar is required to overturn it. Adjustable counterweights shall be placed at the ends of the bases farthest from the uprights so that at each height a force of at least 4 kilograms (8 lbs., 13 oz.) is required to overturn the hurdle.
   2. The measurements of a hurdle shall be the minimum width of 1.04 meters (41″), preferably (but in no case should adjacent hurdles be touching), the extreme base length of 70 centimeters (2′3½″). The top bar shall be 7 centimeters (2¾″) wide and shall be striped.
   3. The height of hurdles shall be either 76 centimeters (30″) or 84 centimeters (33″) as indicated by Figure 1.

b. Height and Distance Specifications
   Recognized distances and heights for hurdle races shall be as indicated in Figure 1.

c. Conduct of Hurdle Competition
   1. All hurdle races will be run in lanes, and the hurdler shall keep to that lane throughout. Hurdlers must attempt to clear every hurdle without trailing a foot alongside the hurdle and without impeding another's progress. A competitor guilty of either of these violations or of deliberately knocking down hurdles by hand or foot shall be disqualified.

2. The hurdles shall be so placed on the track that the feet of the hurdles shall be on the side of the approach of the competitor.
3. The 300 meter (330 yard) hurdles shall be run around one turn.
4. All rules listed under "General Rules of Competition" and "Conduct of the Race" shall also apply to hurdle events.

Distance of Race (age group)	Number of Hurdles	Height of Hurdles	Distance from Start to First Hurdle	Distance Between Hurdles	Distance from Last Hurdle to Finish
50 yds. (9–14)	4	30"(76m)	39'4½" (12m)	26'3" (8m)	31'10½" (9.71m)
50m. (9–14)	4	30"(76m)	39'4½" (12m)	26'3" (8m)	45'11½" (14m)
80 yds. (12–15+)	7	30"(76cm)	42'7¾" (13m)	27'10½" (8.5m)	30'¼" (9.15m)
80m. (12–15+)	8	30"(76cm)	42'7¾" (13m)	27'10½" (8.5m)	24'7¼" (7.5m)
100m. (12–14)	10	30"(76cm)	42'7¾" (13m)	27'10½" (8.5m)	34'5½" (10.5m)
100m. (15–open)	10	33"(84cm)	42'7¾" (13m)	27'10½" (8.5m)	34'5½" (10.5m)
200m. (15–open)	10	30"(76cm)	52'6" (16m)	62'4" (19m)	42'7¾" (13m)
300m. (15–open)	8	30"(76cm)	147'7¼" (45m)	114'10" (35m)	32'9¾" (10m)
400m. (open)	10	30"(76cm)	147'7½" (45m)	114'10" (35m)	131'2¾" (40m)

Note: The 400-meter race is at the same spacing as the men's intermediate race.

Figure 1. Outdoor Hurdle Events Table

SECTION 6. Relays and Shuttle Relay

a. Equipment
   The baton carried in the relay races shall be a smooth hollow tube constructed of a rigid material of one piece weighing not less than 50 grams (1¾ oz.). The length shall not be less than 28 centimeters (11") nor more than 30 centimeters (12"). The circumference shall not be more than 12 centimeters (4¾") nor less than 10 centimeters (4"). The baton is not to be taped. The baton shall be of a color or of a finish so as to be clearly visible.

b. Conduct of Relay Competition
   1. The baton must be carried in the hand throughout the race.
   2. When two or more relay teams are entered in an event by an institution, each team must have a different designation.
   √ 3. Four (4) competitors may be designated for each relay team.

More than one team may be entered for each event. If after a qualifying round a relay competitor suffers an injury or illness that is serious enough to secure a doctor's certificate for withdrawal, that team may substitute any member on the team roster and continue to participate. Only two such substitutions shall be allowed for any relay team.

4. When only one relay team is permitted to run for a team, any member on the team roster may participate in case of injury or withdrawal by an original member of the relay team. If two or more relay teams are entered in an event by one team, any member on the team roster other than the four who were declared to run for each relay team shall be eligible to substitute on any relay team. However, in no case will the four declared personnel for a relay team be allowed to shift from one team to another.

5. At the time of the declaration of entries, the declarer must indicate whether relay teams entered are to compete but designation of the make-up of a relay team need not be made until a designated time before the start of the first round of the event as determined by the meet director or by the rules.

6. The order of running, as differentiated from the composition of the team, may be changed between trial heats and finals in all relay events except in medley relay races. However, in the medley relay, members of the team who have run legs of equal distances may be interchanged (i.e., 100 M legs only may be switched in the 800 M medley relay).

7. No competitor may run more than one leg of a relay.

8. The relay team shall be assigned a lane by draw in all heats and finals.

9. The 800 yard medley relay shall be run in the following order: (110-110-220-440) or 800 meter medley relay (100-100-200-400).

10. The 20 meter (22 yard) exchange zone will be marked at each relay exchange stage. For races of up to 4 × 220 yards, an acceleration zone (international zone) of 10 meters (11 yards) will be marked for outgoing competitors who wish to commence their run prior to the exchange zone. The beginning of this zone shall also be marked in the lanes. In all other relays around the track (4 × 440, etc.) outgoing competitors waiting for the baton must take up positions within the 20 meter exchange zone.

11. In the 800 meter (880 yard) medley relay, competitors may use the acceleration zone (international zone) during the first two exchanges. However, the acceleration zone (international zone) will not be used at the third exchange since the pass is to an outgoing 400 meter (440 yard) runner.

12. The baton must be exchanged within the exchange zone. The baton is considered passed when it is in the hands of the receiver only. It is not the position of the body or limbs of the competitors, but the position of the baton which is decisive.

13. If dropped, the baton must be recovered by the competitor who dropped it. A competitor may step out of the lane or off the track to recover the baton if in so doing she does not interfere with another competitor or gain an advantage. However, if it is dropped during the exchange, either competitor may pick up the baton.

14. The mile relay (4 × 440 yards) or 1600 meter relay (4 × 400 meters) will be run with a three-turn stagger. The first exchange of this relay will be staggered since the second competitor will not break for the inside lane until completing the turn. In races between only two or three teams, a one-turn stagger may be used by the leadoff runner with the break for the inside lane made after completion of the first curve.

15. The two mile relay (4 × 880 yards) or 3200 meter relay (4 × 800 meters) will be run with a one-turn stagger. The leadoff runner may break for the inside lane after completing the first curve at the pole or flag beginning the straightaway.

16. In the 2nd or 3rd exchanges in the mile relay, and all exchanges of the two mile relay, outgoing competitors will occupy the same positions as their incoming teammates hold relative to each other. The leaders will pass in the first lane, second place holders in the second, and so on. Awaiting teammates may slide to the inside position providing interference will not occur.

17. After passing the baton, competitors must continue in their lanes or zones so as to not interfere with other competitors. A competitor impeding a member of another team by running out of position or lane may cause the disqualification of that team.

18. The 800 meter (880 yard) medley relay shall be run in a two-turn stagger. The fourth runner in the 800 meter (880 yard) medley relay may cut for the inside lane as soon as the baton is received,

provided that movement does not interfere with competitors in the inside lane.

19. The relays up to and including 4 × 200 meter shall be run in lanes through the entire distance.

20. The 4 × 100 meter relay shall be run with a two-turn stagger.

21. The 4 × 200 meter relay shall be run with a four-turn stagger.

22. In relays in which the first competitor runs a distance of 440 yards or less, competitors must use starting blocks. In relays in which the competitors run more than 440 yards for the first leg (i.e., 4 × 880 yards, 4 × 800 meters), competitors may not use starting blocks.

23. In relays in which the competitors run more than 440 yards for the first leg (i.e., 4 × 880 yards, 4 × 800 meters), competitors will use the starting procedures for the middle distance races. (See Rule 5, Section 4.)

24. All rules listed under "General Rules of Competition" and "Conduct of the Race" shall also apply to the relay races.

c. Shuttle Relays

1. A competitor, with hands and feet behind the restraining line, shall be touched on the right shoulder by the incoming runner. The competitor may be in an upright position or in a crouch position at the time of the tag. Rules of the start shall apply for each succeeding runner.

   If desired, the exchange zone may be designated by a line four feet ahead of the starting line. The incoming runner is considered to have entered the exchange zone when her torso breaks the plane of this line, and the succeeding runner may then leave the stationary position on the starting line.

2. All rules listed under "General Rules of Competition" and "Conduct of the Race" shall also apply to the shuttle relays.

SECTION 7. Race Walking

a. Race walking is advancing through a progression of steps so taken that unbroken contact with the ground is maintained. The walker must progress in such a manner as to have the lead foot (preferably the heel) make contact with the ground before the rear foot leaves the ground. The leg must be extended (i.e., not bent at the knee) for at least a moment, and the support leg must be extended in the vertically upright position. (See Figures 2 and 3.)

Figure 2
Preferable foot contact

Figure 3
Ideal extended leg position

b. A competitor shall be cautioned by the judge when the mode of progression ceases to comply with Section 7a above. A repetition of the violation shall result in disqualification. Violations include:

    1. Lifting— failure on the part of the race walker to maintain unbroken contact with the ground. See Figure 4.

    2. Creeping—failure on the part of the race walker to fully extend the leg on the stride (Figure 5) or to fully extend the support leg (Figure 6).

c. The race walk should be conducted over a distance of 1600 meters (1 mile) or greater, or a distance established by the meet director or Games Committee.

d. All rules listed under "General Rules of Competition" and "Conduct of the Race" shall also apply to the Race Walk.

Figure 4
"Lifting"

Figure 5   **Figure 6**
"Creeping"

Rule 6. Field Events

SECTION 1. General Rules

a. The order of competition in all qualifying, trial and final rounds shall be drawn by lot.

b. With the exception of high jump, when flights are used, the following procedure shall apply:

1. competitors shall be assigned to flights by lot, working alternately from top to bottom, bottom to top. (See PTO "Determining Flights.")
2. if two competitors from the same team fall in the same flight, one competitor may be exchanged with a competitor of near equivalent order in an adjoining flight.

c. All measurements must be made with a certified steel tape or fiberglass tape or a bar graduated in centimeters or quarter inches for the mark to be submitted for a record. In case of a World Record submission, only measurements from a steel tape graduated in centimeters will be accepted.

d. Distances (except those in discus and javelin competition), if measured in meters, shall always be recorded to the nearest 1 centimeter ($\frac{1}{2}$") below the distance covered, i.e., fractions of less than 1 centimeter ($\frac{1}{2}$") must be ignored. In the case of the discus and javelin throws, distances shall always be recorded in even 2-centimeter (1") units to the nearest unit below.

e. Competitors in all field events shall be allowed 90 seconds from the time the name is called to initiate a trial. Failure to comply within that time period shall be counted as a trial.

f. The number of finalists to be selected in the field events shall correspond with the maximum number of finalists that will be selected for the track events run in lanes. Where there are 8 competitors or fewer, each competitor shall be allowed 6 trials. (Javelin, shot put, discus, long jump.)

g. In the event of a tie for the last qualifying position for finals any or all competitors so tying shall also advance to the finals.

h. Field events shall not be delayed while track events take place unless for reasons of safety. If a competitor is competing in another event— track and/or field—which requires missing the trial in the official order, the Head Judge of the event shall allow that competitor to take trials out of the official order. (See Rule 4, #15.)

i. The levels of the runways and landing areas; throwing areas—shot and discus circles, the javelin runway, and all sectors; and jumping areas—take-offs, pits and runways must all be inspected by an official surveyor. The maximum lateral inclination of the runways for throwing and jumping events shall be 1:100 and the inclination in the running or throwing direction shall not exceed 1:1000.

j. If a suitable warm-up area is available, each competitor may have three practice trials under the supervision of the field events judge immediately prior to the flight. In case there is no warmup area or runway available, a period of general warm-up must be provided for all competitors prior to the commencement of competition by each flight.

k. Once the competition has begun, the competitor is not permitted to use the runway, circle, take-off area or the grounds within the sector for practice with or without an implement. (Exception: Rule 4; 15, 16, 17)

l. Each competitor shall be credited with the best of all jumps or throws either in the preliminary (trials) or final round of competition. If a qualifying round is necessary, performances made during the qualifying will not be used for final placings, but may count as meet or other records.

m. If a competitor is hampered in a trial in a field event, a substitute trial may be awarded at the discretion of the referee.

SECTION 2. Jumping Events General Rules

a. Competitors may not wear shoes which incorporate any spring or device of any kind, nor may they use shoes with the sole and inner sole having an overall thickness in excess of 13 millimeters ($\frac{1}{2}$"). Competitors may not add insoles or other appliances which increase the total thickness of the sole and inner sole above the permitted $\frac{1}{2}$". (See Rule 4, General Rules of Competition.)

b. The use of weights or grips of any kind is strictly prohibited.

c. The head field event judge of either jump will call the order of competitors at the beginning of competition and give instructions concerning the procedures of the competition.

d. Metric measurements are to be used in intercollegiate competition. These shall be recorded to the lesser centimeter. For example, a measurement of 1.856 meters shall be recorded as 1.85 meters. In cases where English measurement is used, measurements shall be recorded to the lesser $\frac{1}{4}$". For example: a measurement of 5'7$\frac{3}{8}$" should be recorded as 5'7$\frac{1}{4}$". A measurement of 19'10$\frac{5}{8}$" should be recorded as 19'10$\frac{1}{2}$".

e. Where there are enough competitors to warrant, it is recommended that the qualifying competition be divided into two or more groups. It is suggested that the size of flights be no larger than 10 in the long jump and 6 in the high jump. The "revolving flight" procedure is suggested for use in the high jump. (See page 179.)

SECTION 3. High Jump

a. Facilities
   1. The distance between the vertical uprights or standards shall not be less than 4.00 meters (13'1½") nor more than 4.04 meters (13'3").
   2. The standards shall be of sufficient height to exceed the maximum height the crossbar can be raised by at least 100 millimeters (4").
   3. The crossbar supports shall be flat and rectangular in shape. They shall be 40 millimeters (1½") wide and 60 millimeters (2½") long and face the opposite standard so that the crossbar will rest along the narrow dimension, and in such a manner that if the crossbar is touched by a competitor it will easily fall to the ground either forward or backward.
   4. There shall be a space of at least 10 millimeters (½") between the end of the crossbar and the standards.

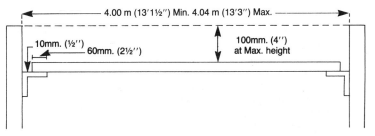

Figure 7. High Jump Uprights, Crossbar and Supports.

   5. The crossbar shall be constructed of wood, metal, fiberglass, or other suitable material. The shape shall be triangular or circular in section.*
      • Each side of the triangular crossbar shall measure 28 millimeters (1⅛").*
      • The diameter of the circular bar shall be at least 25 millimeters (1") but not more than 30 millimeters (1⅛"). The ends of the crossbar shall be constructed in such a way that a flat surface of

---

*Beginning in November 1985 a new rule excluding the use of the triangular crossbar will go into effect.

30×150 millimeters ($1'' \times 6''$) is obtained for placing the bar on the standard supports.

6. The length of the crossbar shall be between 3.98 meters ($13'1''$) and 4.02 meters ($13'2\frac{1}{2}''$) and shall have a maximum weight of 2.0 kilograms (4 lb. $6\frac{1}{2}$ oz.).

7. The landing pit shall have optimal dimensions of 5 meters ($16'4''$) by 3 meters ($9'8\frac{1}{2}''$) and be of a composition which will provide a safe landing. The pit should not be less than 30 centimeters ($12''$) above take-off (minimum). The minimum dimensions of the pit shall be 4 meters ($13'1\frac{1}{2}''$) by 2.44 meters ($8'$).

8. The approach area or apron shall be at least 15 meters ($49'$) in length from any point in its arc of 150 degrees. Where conditions permit, the approach distance shall not be shorter than 18 meters ($59'$).

9. The apron must be level with the point of measurement directly under the crossbar.

b. Conduct of High Jump Competition

1. At the start of the competition, the judge shall announce the starting height and the heights to which the bar will be raised at the end of each round to all competitors as determined prior to competition. Until there is one competitor remaining or there is a tie, the bar should never be raised by less than 2 centimeters after each round. In combined events the raising shall be uniformly 3 centimeters throughout the competition.

2. The initial height of the bar for jumpers in qualifying competition is set by the Games Committee. In a large meet or championship meet where qualifying standards are required, the initial height will be set as follows: take the median height of the jumpers' best marks (submitted for qualifying) and drop 10 centimeters ($4''$). After the first round, the bar is raised by 5 centimeters ($2''$). Subsequently, the bar will be raised by 2 or 3 centimeters ($1''$) increments until the next qualifying standard is reached. If less than twelve (12) competitors achieve the qualifying standard, the finals are filled with enough jumpers to fill the field of 12 from the next lower height. Tie-breaking procedures will not be used in qualifying rounds. All jumpers making the height on their 1st, 2nd or 3rd attempt shall be taken to the final.

3. The initial height of the crossbar in the finals will be set at 10 centimeters ($4''$) below the qualifying standard for the competi-

tion and raised at 5 centimeter (2″) increments until the qualifying standard is reached. At that time, the bar will be raised by 2 or 3 centimeter (1″) increments. (See Exception Rule 8, Sect. 6b, Combined Events.)

4. An accurate measurement of the height of the high jump crossbar shall be taken each time it is raised to a new height, each time a new crossbar replaces a broken one and when the crossbar is replaced on the standards after a miss by a competitor.

5. All measurements must be made with a steel tape, fiberglass tape, or bar graduated in centimeters or quarter inches and shall be made perpendicular from the ground to the lowest part of the upper side of the bar. Any measurement of a new height will be made before competitors attempt such height. In all cases of records, the field referee must check the measurement after the height has been cleared.

6. One surface of the crossbar shall be marked so that the same surface of the crossbar is always facing the same direction.

7. The competitor may place marks on the apron to assist in the run-up and take-off. The marks must be approved by the event judge. The competitor may also place an item such as a handkerchief on the crossbar for sighting purposes.

8. A legal jump is one in which the competitor jumps from one foot.

√9. Failed attempts include:
   a) knocking the crossbar off the supports in an attempt to clear it;
   b) touching the ground or landing area beyond the plane extended by the uprights without clearing the bar;
   c) breaking the vertical plane of the crossbar even when a jump is not attempted;
   d) displacing the crossbar by stumbling against the upright after clearing the bar and landing in the pit;
   e) failure to initiate a jump within 90 seconds after the competitor's name has been called.
   f) a hit bar falling *even* after the competitor has left the pit and/or the landing area (not due to the wind).
   Note: If any athlete, when she jumps, touches the landing area with her foot and in the opinion of the judge no advantage is gained, the jumps should not for that reason be considered a failure.

SECTION 6. Throwing Events General Rules

a. Three trials shall be allowed in the preliminary rounds of competition. Three throws shall be allowed in the final round of competition.

b. All implements used in competition must conform to official standard size, weight, and composition and be officially approved. If so desired, any approved implement may be used by any competitor.

c. In all throwing events from a circle, a competitor must commence the throw from a stationary position. A competitor in a field event shall be disqualified if she uses an implement or equipment that has been illegally altered after having been officially inspected or if she uses an unapproved or illegal implement or equipment. All records, performances, or points scored with the use of such implement or equipment shall be declared null and void.

d. The head field event judge will call the names of the competitors in order of competition as follows: "Brown, Smith and Jones. Brown up."

e. Foul throws shall not be measured.

f. The implement must fall within and not on the sector lines.

g. A competitor may interrupt a trial, lay her implement down, and leave the circle, before returning to a stationary position and beginning a fresh trial—but only if the time consumed between the interruption and resumption of the trial does not exceed 90 seconds.

h. The measurement of each throw shall be made from the nearest mark made by the fall of the implement to the inside of the circumference of the circle, or the arc in the case of the javelin, along a line from the mark made by the implement to the center of the circle (shot, discus) or the center of the circle of which the arc is a part (javelin).

i. In all measurements, the zero end of the tape must be held at the point of the mark made by the implement.

j. The measurement of each throw shall be made immediately after the throw.

k. In the javelin and discus competitions, a distinctive flag or marker shall be provided to mark the best throw of each competitor, and this shall be placed along a line or tape outside the sector lines. A distinctive flag or disc shall also be provided to mark the existing World Record and, when appropriate, the existing American record in each throwing event.

l.   No device of any kind (e.g., the taping of two or more fingers together) which in any way assists a competitor when making a throw shall be allowed. The use of tape on the hand shall not be allowed except in the case of the need to cover an open cut or wound.

m.   The use of gloves is not allowed.

n.   To obtain a better grip, competitors shall be permitted to use an adhesive substance such as resin or a similar substance on their hands only.

o.   A belt of leather or some other suitable material may be worn at the waist by a competitor to protect the spine or back from injury.

p.   A competitor may not spray or spread any substance in the circle, nor on her shoes.

SECTION 7. Shot Put

a. Facilities and Equipment
   1. The put shall be made from a circle 2.135 meters (7′) in diameter. The circle shall be made of band iron, steel, aluminum or other suitable material, the top of which shall be flush with the ground outside. At the middle of the circumference in the front half of the circle a toeboard shall be placed firmly fastened to the ground.
   2. In all official meets the toeboard shall be made of wood or some other suitable material in the shape of an arc, so that the inner edge coincides with the inner edge of the circle, and so that it can be firmly fixed to the ground. The toeboard is 1.21-1.23 meters (4′) long on the inside, 112-116 millimeters (4½″) wide, and 98-102 millimeters (4″) high. The board shall be painted white.
   3. The interior of the circle shall consist of a surface constructed of concrete, asphalt or some other firm, but not slippery, material. The interior surface of this circle shall be level and 20mm ± 6mm (approximately 1 inch) lower than the upper edge of the rim of the circle. A portable circle meeting these specifications is permissible. The surface of the interior circle shall be level with the throwing sector (meeting the requirements of gradient inclination of 1:1000 in the throwing direction).
   4. The putting area shall consist of cinders, grass, or some suitable material on which the shot makes an imprint.
   5. The shot shall be a solid sphere of iron, brass, or any metal not softer than brass, or a shell of such metal filled with lead or other

material. The minimum weight for the college or open division shall be 4 kilograms (8 lbs. 13 oz.); the minimum weight for junior and senior high school girls shall be 8 pounds; the minimum weight for elementary school girls shall be 6 pounds. The minimum diameter shall be 3¾″ and the maximum shall be 4 11/32″. Only a leather-bound or plastic covered indoor shot of the above weights shall be used for indoor meets. (No outdoor shot shall be used for indoor competition.)

b. Conduct of Shot Put Competition

1. To be valid, all puts must fall within the 40° sector lines. A 60° sector is optional for high school competition. These lines 50 millimeters (2″) wide, which form an angle of 40° shall be extended from the center of the circle. The inner edges of these lines shall mark the sector. The ends of the sector lines shall be marked with flags.

2. A fair put shall be one in which no part of the competitor's body touches the top of the toeboard, the circle, or the ground outside the circle.

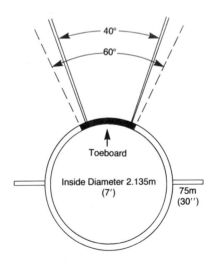

Figure 10. Shot Put Ring

3. The shot shall be put from the shoulder with one hand only. At the time the competitor takes a stance in the ring to commence a put, the shot shall touch or be in close proximity to the chin and the hand shall not be dropped below this position during the action of putting. During the attempt, the shot shall not be brought behind the line of the shoulders.

4. Foul puts will not be measured but will count as a trial. Fouls include:
   a) Putting with both hands.
   b) Dropping the hand below the specified position during the act of putting.
   c) Bringing the shot behind the line of the shoulders.
   d) Stepping on or over the toeboard. (Touching the inside of the stopboard is allowed).
   e) Leaving the circle before the distance has been marked.
   f) Touching the ground with any part of the body outside the circle, after having stepped into the circle and begun to make a throw.
   g) Not leaving the circle from a standing position.
   h) Not leaving the circle from the rear half, which shall be indicated by an imaginary line drawn through the center and marked outside the circle not less than 75 centimeters (30″) on each side.
   i) Putting the shot onto or outside of the sector lines.

5. The measurement shall be taken from the nearest mark made by the fall of the shot to the inside of the circumference of the circle, on a line from such mark by the shot to the center of the circle.

SECTION 8. Discus

a. Facilities and Equipment
   1. The discus shall be thrown from a circle 2.50 meters (8′2½″) in diameter. The circle is 6 millimeters (¼″) in thickness and shall be made of band iron, steel, aluminum or other suitable material which shall be flush with the ground outside. The interior surface of the ring may be constructed of concrete, asphalt or other firm, but not slippery, material. The interior surface of the ring shall be level and 20mm ± 6mm (approximately 1 inch) lower than the upper edge of the rim of the circle.

2. The discus will be constructed of wood or other suitable material, permanently framed with a metal rim, the edge of which shall be rounded in a true circle. Circular plates may be set flush into the center of the sides. The discus may be made without metal plates provided that the equivalent area is flat, and the total weight and other measurements correspond to the following specifications: minimum weight of 1 kilo (2 lbs., 2.7 oz.); outside diameter of metal rim 180mm-182mm (7⅛"-7¼"); diameter of metal plate or flat center area 50mm-57mm (2"-2¼"); thickness of flat center area 37 mm-39mm (approximately 1½"); thickness of metal rim 12mm (½").

3. Each side of the discus shall be identical and shall be made without indentations, projections or sharp edges. The sides shall taper in a straight line from the beginning of the curve of the rim to a circle of a radius 25mm-28.5mm (1") from the center of the discus.

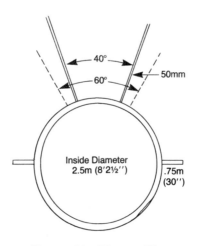

Figure 11. Discus Ring

b. Conduct of Discus Competition
   1. To be valid, all throws must fall within the 40° sector lines. a 60° sector is optional for high school competition. These lines, 50 millimeters (2″) wide, which form an angle of 40° shall be extended from the center of the circle. The inner edges of these lines shall mark the sector. The ends of the sector lines shall be marked with flags.
   2. Foul throws will not be measured but will count as a trial. Fouls include:
      a) Stepping on or over the circle. (Touching the inner face of the marking band is allowed.)
      b) Leaving the circle before the distance has been marked.
      c) Throwing the discus onto or outside of the sector lines.
      d) Letting the discus go in making an attempt.
      e) Touching the ground outside the circle with any part of the body after having stepped into the circle and begun to make a throw.
      f) Not leaving the circle from a standing position.
      g) Not leaving the circle from the rear half, which shall be indicated by an imaginary chalk line drawn through the center and marked outside the circle not less than 75 centimeters (30″) on each side.
   3. The measurement of each throw shall be from the nearest mark made by the fall of the discus to the inside circumference of the circle, on a line from such a mark made by the discus to the center of the circle.
   4. A cage should partially enclose the throwing circle to ensure the safety of inspectors, officials and competitors.

SECTION 9. Javelin

a. Facilities and Equipment
   1. The runway for the javelin throw shall not be more than 36.5 meters (120′), but not less than 30 meters (98′6″). It shall be marked by two parallel lines 4 meters (13′1½″) apart, 5 centimeters (2″) in width, and terminated by a scratch line arc. The throw shall be made from behind an arc of a circle drawn with a radius of 8 meters (26′3″).

THROWING SECTOR

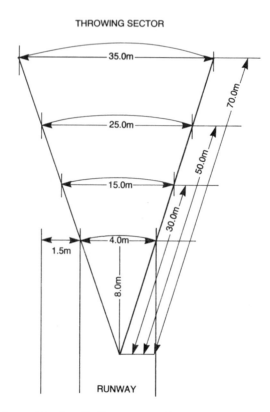

Figure 12. Javelin Runway and Throwing Sector

2. The scratch line arc shall be a board of wood or metal or paint 7 centimeters (2¾″) in width, painted white and shall be flush with the ground.
3. Lines shall be drawn from the extremities of the arc at right angles to the parallel lines marking the runway. These lines shall be 1.5 meters (5′) in length and 7 centimeters (2¾″) in width.

4. The sector is formed by extending the radii through the extremities of the arc up to a distance of 70 meters (229 2/3') depending on the quality of the competition. These lines shall be 7 centimeters (2¾") in width. The ends of the radii lines shall be marked with flags. Distances may be marked at intermediate points, e.g., 30 meters (98½'), 50 meters (164'), 70 meters (229 2/3').

5. The javelin shall be made of metal or solid wood with a metal head. The length shall not be less than 220 centimeters (7'2½") nor more than 230 centimeters (7'6½"). It shall weigh not less than 600 grams (1 lb. 5.16 oz.) inclusive of cord grip. The length of the metal head shall not be less than 25 centimeters (9¾") nor more than 33 centimeters (13"). The distance from the tip of the metal head to the center of gravity shall not be less than 80 centimeters (2'7½") nor more than 95 centimeters (3'1½"). The diameter of the shaft at the thickest point shall not be less than 20 millimeters (¾") nor more than 25 millimeters (1"). The width of the cord grip shall not be less than 14 centimeters (5½") nor more than 15 centimeters (6").

6. The javelin shall have no movable part which shall change its center of gravity.

b. Conduct of Javelin Competition

1. No mark shall be placed on the runway, but competitors may place marks at the side of the runway.

2. The javelin must be held by the grip, with one hand only, so that the little finger is nearest to the point.

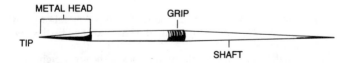

Figure 13. Javelin

3. The javelin shall be thrown over the shoulder or upper part of the throwing arm, and may not be slung or hurled with an underhand motion. Non-orthodox styles are not permitted.

4. Foul throws will not be measured but will count as a trial. Fouls include:
    a) If the competitor touches the scratch line arc with any part of the body or apparel before her throw has been marked.
    b) If a competitor turns completely around so that the competitor's back is toward the throwing area before the javelin has been discharged into the air.
    c) If the javelin lands on or outside the sector lines.
    d) If any part of the javelin other than the tip of the metal head strikes the ground first. (See Figure 13.)
    e) If a competitor fails to leave the runway from behind the scratch line arc and the lines drawn from the extremities of the arc after the throw has been marked.

5. If the javelin breaks at any time during the course of the throw, it shall not count as a trial provided the throw was made in accordance with the rules.

6. Measurements shall be taken at the inner edge of the circumference of the arc. Such measurement shall be made on a line from the nearest mark made by the tip of the metal head of the javelin to the center of the circle of which the arc is a part.

SECTION 10. Softball Throw

a. An official 12-inch softball shall be used.
b. The throw shall be made with either hand, but not with both hands simultaneously.
c. The throw shall be made from the javelin throwing area (see Figure 12), or from behind a scratch line 10 feet long and 2 inches wide. Properly marked, this line shall be a board sunk flush with the ground or a similar line.
d. Stepping on or over the line before the throw has been marked constitutes a foul.
e. A foul throw is not measured but counts as a trial.
f. Measurement shall be taken from the nearest mark made by the fall of the ball to the inside edge of the center of the scratch line.

Rule 7. Indoor Competition

SECTION 1. Conduct of Competition

All general rules of competition shall apply except where stated in Rule 7.

SECTION 2. Determination of Heats and Lanes

Procedures regarding determination of heats and lanes in Rule 5 shall apply. (See Rule 5, Sect. 2.)

SECTION 3. Distance Races

a. If more than 12 competitors are declared for the 1000 meter or 1500 meter runs, trials shall be run. When trials are run, 12 shall be selected for finals. For one day meets with more than 12 competitors, sections (composed of competitors with comparable times) may be run. In the best interest of all concerned, the Games Committee or meet director may schedule these races to be run in sections in lieu of trials if notification is provided in the original schedule. Sections shall be composed of competitors with comparable times.

b. If more than 18 competitors are declared for the 3000 meter (2 mile) or 5000 meter (3 mile) runs, sections shall be run. Sections shall be composed of competitors with comparable times.

c. The 3200 meter (4 × 800) or two mile (4 × 880) relay and the distance medley (800-400-1200-1600; 880-440-¾ mile-mile) will be run with a waterfall start or a one-turn stagger. The lead-off runner may break for the inside lane after completing the first curve at the pole or flat at the beginning of the straightaway.

SECTION 4. Relay and Relay Zone

a. Relay zones are the same as outlined in Rule 5, Section 6, except that no international (fly) zones may be used during any of the relay races. Receivers shall line up in the same relative positions to one another than their teammate holds relative to the other runners as they enter the final turn. The leader will pass in the first lane, second place in the second lane, etc. When no interference is possible, receivers may move into the pole lane.

b. The 1600 meter (4 × 400) or mile (4 × 440) relay will be run with a two-turn stagger. The lead-off runner may break for the inside lane after completing the second curve at the pole or flag beginning at the straightaway.

SECTION 5. Hurdle Placement

To determine placement of hurdles for indoor competition, refer to Figure 14, below.

Distance of Race (age group)	Number of Hurdles	Height of Hurdles	Distance from Start to First Hurdle	Distance between Hurdles	Distance from Last Hurdle to Finish
50 yds. (9-14)	4	30'' (76cm)	39'4½'' (12m)	26'3'' (8m)	31'10½'' (9.71m)
50 m (9-14)	4	30'' (76cm)	39'4½'' (12m)	26'3'' (8m)	45'11½'' (14m)
50 yds. (15-open)	4	33'' (84cm)	42'7'' (13m)	27'10½'' (8.5m)	23'8'' (7.23m)
50 m (15-open)	4	33'' (84cm)	42'7'' (13m)	27'10½'' (8.5m)	37'8'' (11.5m)
55 m (open)	5	33'' (84cm)	42'7'' (13m)	27'10½'' (8.5m)	26'3'' (8m)
60 yds. (open)	5	33'' (84cm)	42'7'' (13m)	27'10½'' (8.5m)	25'10¼'' (7.88m)
60 m (open)	5	33'' (84cm)	42'7'' (13m)	27'10½'' (8.5m)	42'7'' (13m)
70 yds. (open)	6	33'' (84cm)	42'7'' (13m)	27'10½'' (8.5m)	27' (8.25m)

Figure 14. Indoor Hurdle Event Table

SECTION 6. Determination of Number of Finalists in Field Events

Qualify one more than places being scored in the meet.

SECTION 7. Shot Put

a. Portable circles meeting specifications is permissible. (See Rule 6, Section 7a)
b. Only a leather-bound or plastic covered indoor shot shall be used. (See Rule 6, Section 7a5.)

Rule 8. Combined Events: Triathlon, Pentathlon, Heptathlon

SECTION 1. The triathlon consists of three events. The order of the events for the triathlon is 50 or 60 meter hurdles, shot put, high jump.

SECTION 2. The pentathlon is governed by the rules listed below and is scored in accordance with the International Pentathlon Table[1] or IAAF.[2]

SECTION 3. The pentathlon for girls and women consists of five events:
   50 yard/100 meter hurdle
   8 pound/4 kilo shot put
   High jump
   Running long jump
   800 meter run
a. The order of events shall be: hurdles, shot put, high jump, long jump, 800 meters.
b. The pentathlon may be held in two sessions in one day or on two consecutive days.
c. The first session shall consist of hurdles, shot put and high jump. The second session shall consist of long jump and 800 meters.

SECTION 4. The pentathlon may be included in an official track and field meet for girls and women.
a. The pentathlon for junior high (Ages 12-13-14) shall include the following events:

50-yard hurdles	Running long jump
8-lb. shot put	800-meter run
High jump	

b. The pentathlon for high school (Ages 15 and over) and college and open shall include the following events:

100-meter hurdles	Running long jump
8 lb./4 kilo shot put	800-meter run
High jump	

---

[1] Athletic Congress, 3400 W. 86th St., Indianapolis, IN 46268, or
[2] IAAF, 1971 (no later edition).

SECTION 5. The Heptathlon consists of 7 events. The order of events for the Heptathlon is:

First Day: 100 meter hurdles, high jump, shot put, 200 meter

Second Day: long jump, javelin, 800 meter

SECTION 6. Unless otherwise indicated below, all of the rules which govern the individual events apply when these events are included in the triathlon, pentathlon, and heptathlon.

a. At least a ½ hour rest shall be allowed each competitor between consecutive events. Competition may begin on a subsequent event prior to ½ hour after a previous event with the approval of *all* participants.

b. In included field events, when more than one flight is required, a maximum of 30 minutes shall be allowed between the last attempt of the previous flight and the beginning of competition in the next flight except in the high jump. (See Rule 6, Sect. 2e.) In the hurdles, a maximum of 10 minutes shall be allowed between flights. (This rule is to ensure, rather than limit, adequate warmup time.) Competition may begin on a subsequent flight prior to 30 minutes (10 minutes in the hurdles) after the previous flight with the approval of *all* participants. Any athlete may demand the maximum.

c. When more than one flight is required in events, the composition of flights and the scheduled time of each flight shall be posted prior to the beginning of the pentathlon competition, except that the composition of flights in the 800 meters shall be determined prior to the start of that event.

√d. In running events and hurdles, each competitor shall be timed by three timekeepers independently and, if possible, a fully automatic timing device. The most frequent or middle time is the official time. If fully automatic timing is used, time is recorded in increments of 1/100th second. (Electric stopwatches do not qualify as fully automatic timing.) Hand timing shall be recorded to the next longer 1/10th second. <u>One system of timing shall be used throughout the competition.</u>

√e. In running events and hurdles, a competitor shall be disqualified after *three false starts* but may continue to participate in other events.

f. In field events, except for the high jump, each competitor shall be allowed three trials only. (See Rule 6, Sect. 3b.)

g. A competitor failing to start an event shall be disqualified from further events and final placing and scoring. A competitor who has failed to complete an event successfully or who has been disqualified, will receive no points for that event.

h. An athlete disqualified for fouling a competitor in any event shall be permitted to compete in the remaining events unless the Referee shall rule that mere loss of points is not sufficient penalty.

i. Scoring shall be according to IAAF Women's Scoring Tables (1971) Edition or 1975 update) (See Scoring Tables, pages 100-120.)

j. Ties:
   1. If two or more competitors are tied (points and place), the winner shall be the competitor with the highest number of points in a majority of events.
   2. If this does not resolve the tie, the winner shall be the competitor with the highest number of points in any one event.

k. If the number of competitors warrants it, the competitors may be divided into groups of not less than 6 nor more than 10, drawn by lot. These groupings shall continue throughout the competition, except the high jump and 800 meters. The order of competition within each group shall be drawn by lot.

l. Flights in the high jump shall be determined by the "best high jump" marks submitted on entry blanks; the best in one flight, next best in another flight, etc. The order of competition of flights and within flights shall be drawn by lot. (See Rule 6, Sect. 2e.)

m. The starting height for the high jump shall be determined by the competitors. Throughout the competition the bar shall be raised at 3 centimeter (1⅛') increments. Competitors may begin jumping at any height and may jump at their decision at any subsequent height.

n. In hurdles and running events, flights may have 3 or more but never less than 2 competitors. The composition and order of flights in the hurdles shall be drawn by lot. The composition of flights in the 800 meters shall be determined by place after the first four events; the top placers in one flight, the next best placers in another flight, etc. Lanes shall be drawn by lot. The order of flights in the 800 meters shall be drawn by lot.

o. Prior to the first flight in each running event, the starter shall give specific information, and a demonstration of how the start will be given.

p. For record or compilation purposes in outdoor competitions, average wind velocity must be measured and recorded for the hurdles and long jump. Maximum allowable readings in pentathlon only are 4 meters per second (8.94 miles per hour, 787.4 feet per minute).

Rule 9. Cross-country Running

SECTION 1. The Course

The "official" length of the cross-country course shall be as follows:

Age	Distance
9-10-11	Up to 2000 meters (1 mile)
12-13-14	2000-3000 meters (1.5 mile)
15 and over	2000-5000 meters (1.5 to 2 miles)
College and open	3000-7000 meters (2 to 5 miles)

However, by mutual consent of the coaches involved, the distance may be set at a different distance.

A cross-country course should incorporate as many of the following features as possible:

a. Have a distance which is measured over the shortest path that the athletes can run.

b. Be basically flat with small hills and undulations, plus at least one challenging hill not to exceed a 30 degree slope plus an incline just prior to the finish of the race.

c. Provide for both the needs of the runners and the view of fans. Figure eight clover leaf, one mile loops or switchbacks that best suit the terrain available should be considered.

d. Have the start and finish within 200 meters (220 yards) of one another and preferably at the same place. The start and finish of the race may be within an athletic stadium and it may cross paving.

e. Have timers stationed at each 800 meter (880 yard) mark along the course who read split times to all the runners.

f. Have the first turn be between 300 and 400 meters (330-440 yards) from the start. It should not be a sharp turn but rather a very gradual, wide turn. Also the finish should include a straightaway of between 300 and 400 meters (330-440 yards).

g. Be 10 meters (30 feet) wide at the narrowest place.

h. Be marked by a solid continuous chalk line along the shortest distance.

i. Have turns that shall be flagged by a single flag at least 1 meter (3 feet) in height—ideally 1.5 meters (5 feet)—which indicates the inside edge of the course and the direction of the route:

Red—left turn

Yellow—right turn

Turn flags shall be immediately followed by at least two blue directional flags to indicate the continuous path of the course. Runners should be warned to stay on the course.

j. Have signs 1 meter (3 feet) in height to indicate each half mile (1½, 1, 1½, 2, etc.) or 800 meters (800, 1600, 2400, 3200, etc.) depending on whether the course is English or metric.

k. Have a course inspector stationed at every point where confusion may result due to the intricacies of the particular course.

l. Be planned in such a way as to avoid the following hazards along the course:

hidden holes

low stumps

low branches (at least 8 feet off ground)

narrow or swinging bridges

deep ditches

confusing turns or markings

concrete or asphalt surfaces

hazards caused by automobiles, bicycles, horses, etc.

hills too steep to climb in inclement weather

deep sand or loose gravel

barbed-wire fences

stairs

gates

SECTION 2. Conduct of Race

a. On the command "Set," all competitors will immediately move to their set positions. A runner who so fails to comply with this command within a reasonable time shall be charged with a false start.

b. A competitor leaving the mark before the gun is fired shall be charged with a false start. Any competitor making 2 false starts shall be disqualified from the race. A false start shall be called if a competitor leaves the mark and/or is in motion after the "Set" but before the shot is fired.

c. A competitor shall make an honest effort to qualify or place. Intentionally taking two false starts, not leaving the starting line after a legitimate start, or not attempting to run the race after reporting are examples of a lack of honest effort. If an honest effort is not made, the competitor shall be disqualified from the race.

d. Competitors shall be recalled if a runner is jostled and falls or is placed at a distinct disadvantage while in the first 100 yards of the course.

e. Competitors shall be prepared to run the race in such a manner as to ensure their best effort and at the same time permit their opponents equal opportunities for fair competition. Competitors displaying unsporting conduct during the competition shall be disqualified. Examples of actions which shall result in disqualification follow:
   - jostling, cutting across the path, or obstructing another runner so as to impede progress. Direct contact is not necessary; any action that causes an opponent to break stride or lose momentum can lead to disqualification.
   - veering to the right or left on the final straightaway so as to impede a challenging runner and/or force that runner to run a greater distance.
   - forcing way between two leading runners, making direct contact so as to impede the progress of either.
   - leaving the course.
   - holding the hands of a teammate during the race or at the finish.
   - impeding the progress of a runner by deliberate "boxing" by two or more competitors. (This does not include the unintentional "boxes" that frequently occur during the course of the competition.)

f. Competitors must run the marked course.

g. A runner must pass through the funnel and the entire finish chute exiting at the rear in order to be officially counted. (Refer to PTO Section for competitors unable to exit the chute.)

h. Any violation of Rule 9, Section 2 may result in disqualification.

SECTION 3. Scoring

A cross-country team may consist of 5 to 12 runners. The first 7 positions count in the competition with only the first 5 scoring team points. The first runner completing the course will receive 1 point, the second 2 points, the third 3 points and so on. The team score shall be determined by totaling the points scored by the first 5 finishers of each team. The team which scores the smaller number of points is the winner. While the sixth and seventh finishers of a team do not score points toward their team's total, their places, if better than those of any of the first 5 of an opposing team, result in an increased (poorer) score for the opposing team. If fewer than 5 competitors (or any number specified by the meet committee) of a team finish, the places of all members of the team shall be disregarded.

Competitors who tie in the race shall have their points divided between them. Ties between teams shall be resolved in favor of the team whose last scoring member (the 5th place competitor) finishes nearer the first place. In such cases where the 5th place runners of the tied teams may have tied, the relative positions of the 4th place competitors will determine the winner.

SECTION 4. Equipment

For dual and small invitational cross-country meets the host coach will need the following equipment: envelopes (for quick score cards) paper clips or safety pins, pencils, magic markers, starting gun and shells, whistle, towels, measuring wheel, 300 feet measuring tape, awards (trophies, medals), blackboard, folding chairs, table, course marking flags (blue, yellow & red), distance (½, 1, and 2 miles), clipboards, lime and liner, posts and post driver, rope, score sheet, bull horn, runners' identification cards, stopwatches.

SECTION 5. Finish Chutes

a. Single Chute
   The finish line should be located at the end of a long straightaway on very level and even ground. The finish line should be a 30 foot line at right angle to the course line. At each end of the finish line should be a steel post and extending back from the line a funnel should be formed using steel posts and rope. The funnel should end with a 4 foot wide

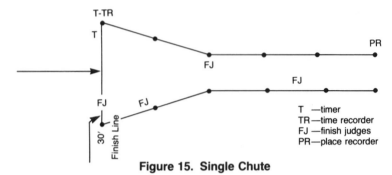

Figure 15. Single Chute

chute that is at least 50 feet long and marked off by steel posts and rope.

1. At least two running watches shall be kept at the finish line to guard against a single watch malfunctioning, and to ensure accurate times for all.
2. Timers shall not be responsible for recording times or finish places.
3. There shall be a time recorder and one or more place recorders.
4. At least one finish judge shall be positioned opposite the timers and recorders to determine positions in close finishes.

Note: See page 203 for Techniques of Cross-country Officiating.

b. Multiple Chute

Multiple chutes are used in large meets to avoid the stacking up of runners at the finish line.

Direct competitors, in order of finish, into chute #1. When it has become full it may be roped or closed off. Chute #2 now becomes the "active" chute as competitors are directed into it. This procedure is followed through chutes #3, #4, etc. Meanwhile, the recorder will be listing the order of finish of the competitors in chute #1*, emptying the chute simultaneously. (When the chute has been emptied it may be used as chute #4 for subsequent finishers.) The recorder proceeds to successive chutes, recording the order of finish.

---

*In large meets it might be wise to assign a recorder to *each* chute. This will greatly expedite the emptying of chutes, thus accommodating more runners and decreasing the possibility of stacking.

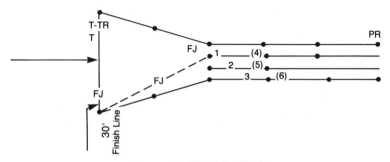

Figure 16. Multiple Chute

Rule 10. Records

SECTION 1.

National records shall be recognized in the events and divisions as listed under Rule 1. There shall be three categories of national records: intercollegiate, junior college, high school.

SECTION 2.

The following provisions shall apply to all track and field records:

a. No records shall be acceptable unless made in a bona fide competition open to two or more schools or colleges and conducted in accordance with NAGWS Rules, and unless all official standards for that event have been met.

b. Records made in heats or qualifying trials will be accepted. In case of a record made in a dead heat or tie, each competitor so tying shall be entitled to the record.

c. No record claimed for any event in which time is taken shall be allowed unless it has been timed by official timers in accordance with the Techniques of Officiating Section.

d. A race must be stated to be over one distance only and all competitors shall compete at that distance. In order for an athlete to be credited with a record in a shorter distance, she must compete the full distance for which the race has been fixed.

e. <u>Records may be set on tracks with more than 8 lanes as long as the radius of the outside lane does not exceed 60 meters.</u>

f. For all records in events up to and including 200 meters (220 yards), and for the running long jump, information on wind conditions should be provided.

   1. An anemometer shall be placed 1.22 meters (4′) above the ground and no more than 2 meters (6′7″) from the edge of the track, midway between the start and finish lines facing the starting line.

   2. If the average velocity of the wind, measured in the direction of the running behind the competitor, either directly, or in a slanting direction, exceeds 2 meters per second, (6′6 2/3″) per second or 393.7 feet per minute or 4.463 miles per hour), the record will not be accepted.

   3. The events for which the wind will be measured (after the gun has been fired) are as follows:

     a) 100 meters (100 yards)—10 seconds

     b) 100 meter (100 yard) hurdles—13 seconds

     c) 200 meters-curve (220 yards-curve)—the average wind shall be measured for a period of 10 seconds commencing when the runners enter the straightaway.

   4. In the long jump an anemometer shall be placed no more than 20 meters (65′7½″) from the take-off board facing the jumper and no farther than 2 meters (6′7″) from the runway at a height of 1.22 meters or 4′ above the ground. The wind shall be measured for a period of 5 seconds when the competitor starts her approach.

g. The equipment used in field events must have been weighed by weighing and measuring devices approved by the Bureau of Weights and Measures. Records in field events must be measured by two field judges and the referee using a *steel* tape or bar graduated in centimeters.

h. No record claimed for the discus, javelin, shot put, basketball or softball throws shall be allowed unless it has been made with an implement which complies with the specifications for official implements, and it must also be certified as to weight, measurement, and material on the date of completion.

SECTION 3.

A national record application shall be accepted for consideration by the Track and Field Committee if the record application form(s) (see Appendix G) submitted is properly certified by referee, judges, timers, and all other necessary officials concerning all pertinent information as follows:

a. Meet and location
b. Time of day and date
c. State of weather
d. Condition of track or field (surface type)
e. Force and direction of wind
f. Level or gradient of ground
g. Correctness of distance run, announced time, and distance or height
h. Specifications of weight, measurement, and material of implement
i. Printed program of meet
j. Complete results of event
k. Photofinish photograph when automatic electrical time keeping was the official recorder of the event.
l. Signatures of referee, meet director and coach.

RULES INTERPRETER

All questions regarding interpretations of these rules should be addressed to:

NELL JACKSON
West Gymnasium
State University of New York
Binghamton, NY 13901

(A self-addressed, stamped envelope should be included.)

Girls' and Women's
Track and Field Records

I.A.A.F. Women's World Records as of January 1st, 1983

100m	10.88	Marlies Oelsner (now Göhr)	(GDR)	Dresden	1.7.77
200m	21.71	Marita Koch	(GDR)	Karl-Marx Stadt	10.6.79
400m	48.15	Marita Koch	(GDR)	Athens	8.9.82
800m	1:53.43	Nadyezhda Olizarenko	(URS)	Moscow	27.7.80
1500m	3:52.47	Tatyana Kazankina	(URS)	Zürich	13.8.80
3000m	8:26.78	Svetlana Ulmasova	(URS)	Kiev	25.7.82
5000m	15:08.26	Mary Decker-Tabb	(USA)	Eugene, USA	5.6.82
10,000m	31:35.3	Mary Decker-Tabb	(USA)	Eugene, USA	17.7.82
1 Mile	4:17.44	Maricica Puica	(RUM)	Rieta, Italy	16.9.82
Marathon:					
best perf.	2:25:28.7	Alison Roe	(NZL)	New York	25.10.81
100m H.	12.36	Grazyna Rabsztyn	(POL)	Warsaw	13.6.80
400m H.	54.28	Karin Rossley	(GDR)	Jena	18.5.80

Walks

5km Walk	22.41.4	Alexandra Deverinskaya	(URS)	Bergen	15.5.82
10km Walk	46.42.6	Susan Cook	(AUS)	Adelaide	23.5.82

Relays

4 × 100m R	41.60	GDR (Müller, Wöckel, Auerswald, Göhr)	(GDR)	Moscow	1.8.80
4 × 200m R	1:28.15	GDR (Göhr, Müller, Wöckel, Koch)	(GDR)	Jena	9.8.80
4 × 400m R	3:19.04	GDR (Siemon, Busch, Ruebsam, Koch)	(GDR)	Athens	11.9.82
4 × 800m R	7:52.3	URS (Providokhina, Gerasimova, Styrkina, Kazankina)	(URS)	Podolsk	16.8.76

Field Events

High Jump	2.02	Ulricke Meyfarth	(FRG)	Athens	8.9.82
Long Jump	7.20	Vali Ionescu	(RUM)	Bucharest	1.8.82
Shot Put	22.45	Ilona Slupianek	(GDR)	Potsdam	11.5.82
Discus	71.80	Maria Petkova	(BUL)	Sofia	13.7.80
Javelin	74.20	Sofia Sakarafa	(GRE)	Khania	26.9.82

Combined Event

Heptathlon	6772 pts	Ramona Neubert	(GDR)	Halle, GDR	19/20.6.82

NATIONAL ASSOCIATION FOR GIRLS & WOMEN IN SPORT

Women's Track and Field World Records (Approved by the I.A.A.F. as of December 31st, 1982)

100m	10.88	Marlies Gohr, GDR	Dresden, GDR	July 1, 1977
	10.88 p	Marlies Gohr, GDR	Karl-Marx-Stadt, GDR	July 9, 1982
200m	21.71	Marita Koch, GDR	Karl-Marx-Stadt, GDR	June 10, 1979
400m	46.16	Marita Koch, GDR	Athens, Greece	Sept. 8, 1982
800m	1:53.43	Nadyezhda Olizaryenko, USSR	Moscow, USSR	July 27, 1980
1500m	3:52.47	Tatyana Kazankina, USSR	Zurich, Switz.	Aug. 13, 1980
1 Mile	4:17.44	Maricica Puica, Rumania	Rieti, Italy	Sept. 16, 1982
3000m	8:26.78	Svyetlana Ulmasova, USSR	Kiev, USSR	July 25, 1982
5000m	15:08.26	Mary Decker Tabb, USA	Eugene, OR	June 5, 1982
10,000m	31:35.3	Mary Decker Tabb, USA	Eugene, OR	July 16, 1982
100m H.	12.36	Grazyna Rabsztyn, Poland	Warsaw, Poland	June 13, 1980
400m H.	54.28	Karin Rossley, GDR	Jene, GDR	May 17, 1980

Relay Events

400m	41.60	GDR (Marlies Gohr, Romy Muller, Barbel Wockel, Marita Koch)	Moscow, USSR	Aug. 1, 1980
800m	1:28.15	GDR (Romy Muller, Barbel Wockel, Ingrid Auerswald, Marlies Gohr)	Jena, GDR	Aug. 9, 1980
1600m	3:19.04	GDR (Kerstin Siemon, Sabine Busch, Dagmar Rubsam, Marita Koch)	Athens, Greece	Sept. 11, 1982
3200m	7:52.3	USSR (Tatyana Providokhina, Vera Gerasimova, Svetlana Styrkina, Tatyana Kazankina)	Podolsk, USSR	Aug. 16, 1976

Field Events

High Jump	2.02m (6'7½")	Ulrike Meyfarth, FRG	Athens, Greece	Sept. 8, 1982
Long Jump	7.20m (23'7½")	Vali Ionescu, Rumania	Bucharest, Rumania	Aug. 1, 1982
Shot Put	22.45m (73'8")	Ilona Slupianek, GDR	Potsdam, GDR	May 11, 1980
Discus Throw	71.80m (235'7")	Maria Vergova, Bulgaria	Sofia, Bulgaria	July 13, 1980
Javelin Throw	74.20m (243'5")	Sofia Sakorafa, Greece	Canea, Greece	Sept. 26, 1982

Multiple Event

Heptathlon	6772 points	Ramona Neubert, GDR	Halle, GDR	June 19-20, 1982

American Records (Approved by T.A.C. as of December 31st, 1982)

American Outdoor Records

Event	Time	Athlete	Location	Date
100m	10.90	Evelyn Ashford, Medalist T.C.	Colo. Springs, CO	July 22, 1981
200m	21.83	Evelyn Ashford, USA	Montreal, Canada	Aug. 24, 1979
400m	50.62	Rosalyn Bryant, USA	Montreal, Canada	July 28, 1976
800m	1:57.9	Madeline Manning, USA	College Park, MD	Aug. 7, 1976
1500m	3:59.43	Mary Decker, Athletics West	Zurich, Switz.	Aug. 13, 1980
1 Mile	4:18.08	Mary Decker Tabb, Athletics West	Paris, France	July 9, 1982
2000m	5:38.9	Mary Decker Tabb, Athletics West	Oslo, Norway	July 7, 1982
3000m	8:29.71	Mary Decker Tabb, Athletics West	Oslo, Norway	July 7, 1982
5000m	15:08.26	Mary Decker Tabb, Athletics West	Eugene, OR	June 5, 1982
10,000m	31:35.3	Mary Decker Tabb, Athletics West	Eugene, OR	July 16, 1982
100m H.	12.79	Stephanie Hightower, USA	Karl-Marx-Stadt, GDR	July 10, 1982
400m H.	56.16	Esther Mahr, USA	Sittard, Neth.	Aug. 15, 1980

Relay Events

Event	Time	Team	Location	Date
400m	42.29	National Team (Alice Brown, Florence Griffith, Randy Givens, Diane Williams)	Karl-Marx-Stadt, GDR	July 9, 1982
400m	43.39	Shaklee T.C. (Alice Brown, Florence Griffith, Valerie Briscoe, Jeannette Bolden)	Sacramento, CA	June 21, 1981
800m	1:32.6	National Team (Wanda Hooker, Karen Hawkins, Chandra Cheeseborough, Brenda Morehead)	Bourges, France	June 24, 1979
800m/880y	1:35.9	Tennessee State U. (Diana Hughes, Patricia Hunter, Ina Davis, Barbara Montgomery)	Knoxville, TN	Apr. 14, 1973
1600m	3:22.81	National Team (Debra Sapenter, Sheila Ingram, Pam Jiles, Rosalyn Bryant)	Montreal, Canada	July 31, 1976
1600m	3:28.68	Los Angeles Naturite T.C. (Sharon Dabney, Denean Howard, Sherri Howard, Rosalyn Bryant)	Knoxville, TN	June 19, 1982

3200m	8:19.9	National Team (Robin Campbell, Bourges, France Joetta Clark, Chris Mullen, Essie Kelley)	June 24, 1979
3200m	8:31.4	Oral Roberts T.C. (Robinson, Walnut, CA Brown, Kim Neall, Madeline Manning)	June 14, 1979
2 Miles	8:34.44	Los Angeles T.C. (Kathy Costello, Roma Antoniewicz, Lauri Mullins, Julie Brown)	June 12, 1976
800m mdly	1:36.79	Wilt's A.C. (Brenda Morehead, Knoxville, TN Jeanette Bolden, Alice Brown, Arlise Emerson)	June 20, 1982
4000m dist mdly	11:08.7	U. of Virginia (Linda Nicholson, Philadelphia, PA Lisa Garrett, Vivian Scruggs, Jill Haworth)	Apr. 23, 1981

Field Events

High Jump	1.98m (6'6")	Coleen Sommer, USA	Durham, NC	June 26, 1982
Long Jump	7.00m (22'11¾")	Jodi Anderson, L.A. Naturite	Eugene, OR	June 28, 1980
Shot Put	19.09m (62'7¾")	Maren Seidler, San Jose Stars	Walnut, CA	June 16, 1979
Discus Throw	63.22m (207'5")	Lorna Griffin, AM Council Ath.	Long Beach, CA	May 24, 1980
Javelin Throw	69.32m (227'5")	Kate Schmidt, Pacific Coast Club	Furth, FRG	Sept. 10, 1977

Multiple Event

Heptathlon	6458 points	Jane Frederick, Athletics West	Goleta, CA	July 17-18, 1982

All-comers Outdoor Records

200m	22.17	Merlene Ottey, L.A. Naturite	Knoxville, TN	June 20, 1982
400m	50.78	Elena Korban, USSR	Indianapolis, IN	July 2, 1982
800m	1:57.0	Tatyana Providokhina, USSR	College Park, MD	Aug. 7, 1976
1500m	4:00.3	Tatyana Kazankina, USSR	College Park, MD	Aug. 6, 1976
1 Mile	4:23.5	Mary Decker, unat.	Philadelphia, PA	June 30, 1979
2000m	5:43.96	Monica Joyce, San Diego State	San Diego, CA	Apr. 30, 1982
3000m	8:27.12	Lyudmila Bragina, USSR	College Park, MD	Aug. 7, 1976
100m H.	12.86	Deby LaPlante, San Diego St.	Walnut, CA	June 16, 1979
	12.86	Stephanie Hightower, LA Naturite	Knoxville, TN	June 19, 1982
400m H.	55.87	Anna Kastetskaya, USSR	Indianapolis, IN	July 3, 1982
400m R	42.47	National Team (Alice Brown, Florence Griffith, Randy Givens, Diane Williams)	Indianapolis, IN	July 2, 1982

Event	Mark	Holder	Location	Date
800m R	1:33.40	U.C.L.A. (Jeanette Bolden, Florence Griffith, Oralee Fowler, Deann Gutowski)	Walnut, CA	Apr. 26, 1981
1600m R	3:25.02	National Team (Rosalyn Bryant, LeShon Nedd, Diane Dixon, Denean Howard)	Durham, NC	June 27, 1982
880y mdly	1:37.7	Tennessee State U. (Brenda Morehead, Ernestine Davis, Chandra Cheeseborough, Deborah Jones)	Los Angeles, CA	June 9, 1978
Shot Put	21.22m (69'7½")	Nadyezhda Chizhova, USSR	Durham, NC	July 6, 1974
Discus Throw	69.34m (227'6")	Galina Savinkova, USSR	Indianapolis, IN	July 2, 1982
Javelin Throw	66.58m (218'5")	Anna Verouli, Greece	Eugene, OR	Sept. 25, 1982

American Junior Records

Event	Mark	Holder	Location	Date
100m	11.13	Chandra Cheeseborough, TN St.	Eugene, OR	June 21, 1976
200m	22.77	Chandra Cheeseborough, USA	Mexico City, Mex.	Oct. 16, 1975
400m	50.87	Denean Howard, L.A. Naturite	Knoxville, TN	June 20, 1982
800m	2:00.07	Kim Gallagher, East	Indianapolis, IN	July 24, 1982
1500m	4:16.8	Francie Larrieu, USA	Stuttgart, FRG	July 31, 1969
	4:16.8	Polly Plumer, Univ. H.S., Irvine	Los Angeles, CA	May 16, 1982
	4:16.6 p	Kim Gallagher, Upper Dublin HS	Villanova, PA	June 12, 1982
1 Mile	4:35.24	Polly Plumer, Univ. H.S., Irvine	Los Angeles, CA	May 16, 1982
3000m	9:08.6	Lynn Bjorklund, USA	Kiev, USSR	July 5, 1975
5000m	16:34.7	Kim Gallagher, Upper Dublin H.S.	Ft. Washington, PA	June 12, 1979
10,000m	34:54.8	Roxanne Bier, San Jose Cindergals	Los Angeles, CA	June 8, 1978
100m H.	12.95	Candy Young, unat.	Walnut, CA	June 16, 1979
400m H.	58.18	Gayle Kellon, USA	Barquisimeto, Ven.	July 31, 1982
400m R	44.07	National Team (Monica Taylor, Denean Howard, Zelda Johnson, Janet Davis)	Barquisimeto, Ven.	July 31, 1982
1600m R	3:34.68	National Team (Gayle Kellon, Nedrea Rodgers, Gervaise McGraw, Maxine Underwood)	Barquisimeto, Ven.	Aug. 1, 1982
High Jump	1.89m (6'2¼")	Kym Carter, East H.S., Wichita	Wichita, KS	Apr. 24, 1982
Long Jump	6.60m (21'8")	Carol Lewis, Willingboro H.S., NJ	Philadelphia, PA	July 17, 1980
Shot Put	15.96m (42'4½")	Natalie Kaaiawahia, Fullerton H.S.	Norwalk, CA	May 28, 1981
Discus Throw	56.06m (183'11")	Leslie Deniz, Gridley H.S., CA	Lancaster, CA	July 3, 1980
Javelin Throw	60.56m (198'8")	Barbara Friedrich, Manasquan H.S., NJ	W. Long Branch, NJ	June 4, 1967
Heptathlon	5405 points	Sharon Hatfield, Ftn. Valley H.S., CA	Los Angeles, CA	June 25-26, 1982

American Indoor Records

Track Events

Event	Time	Name	Location	Date
50y	5.80	Jeanette Bolden, Wilt's A.C.	Toronto, Canada	Jan. 29, 1980
50m	6.13 p	Jeanette Bolden, U.C.L.A.	Edmonton, Canada	Feb. 21, 1981
60y	6.54	Evelyn Ashford, Medalist T.C.	New York, NY	Feb. 26, 1982
60m	7.21	Jeanette Bolden, U.C.L.A.	Tokyo, Japan	Mar. 21, 1981
300y	34.07	Rosalyn Bryant, Muhammad Ali T.C.	Lincoln, NE	Feb. 2, 1980
	34.07	Randy Givens, Florida State	Cedar Falls, IA	Mar. 12, 1982
300m	37.98	Robin Jackson, U. of Wisconsin	Pocatello, ID	Mar. 14, 1981
	37.54 p	Janet Dodson, Morgan State	Morgantown, WV	Mar. 6, 1982
400m	53.31	Gwen Gardner, LA Mercurettes	New York, NY	Feb. 8, 1980
440y	53.5	Rosalyn Bryant, LA Mercurettes	New York, NY	Jan. 28, 1977
500y	1:03.3	Rosalyn Bryant, LA Mercurettes	San Diego, CA	Feb. 18, 1977
500m	1:11.7 p	Delisa Walton, Tennessee	Louisville, KY	Feb. 9, 1980
500m	1:11.8	Rosalyn Bryant, LA Mercurettes	Inglewood, CA	Feb. 4, 1977
(11-lap)				
600y	1:17.38	Delisa Walton, U. of Tenn.	Cedar Falls, IA	Mar. 13, 1982
600y	1:19.3	Robin Campbell, Sport Int'l.	Toronto, Canada	Feb. 15, 1974
(11-lap)				
600m	1:26.56	Delisa Walton, U. of Tenn.	Pocatello, ID	Mar. 14, 1981
800m	1:58.9	Mary Decker, Athletics West	San Diego, CA	Feb. 22, 1980
880y	1:59.7	Mary Decker, Athletics West	San Diego, CA	Feb. 22, 1980
1000y	2:23.8	Mary Decker, Colorado T.C.	Inglewood, CA	Feb. 3, 1978
1000m	2:40.2	Francie Larrieu, Pacific Coast	Los Angeles, CA	Jan. 18, 1975
1500m	4:00.8	Mary Decker, Athletics West	New York, NY	Feb. 8, 1980
1 Mile	4:20.5	Mary Decker Tabb, Athletics West	San Diego, CA	Feb. 19, 1982
3000m	8:47.3	Mary Decker Tabb, Athletics West	Inglewood, CA	Feb. 6, 1982
2 Miles	9:37.03	Joan Hansen, Athletics West	New York, NY	Feb. 26, 1982
50y H.	6.37 p	Deby LaPlante, D.C. Striders	Toronto, Canada	Feb. 10, 1978
50m H.	6.95	Candy Young, Beaver Falls, PA	Edmonton, Canada	Feb. 3, 1979
60y H.	7.37	Stephanie Hightower, LA Naturite	New York, NY	Feb. 12, 1982
	7.37	Candy Young, Fairleigh Dick	New York, NY	Feb. 12. 1982
60m H.	8.04	Stephanie Hightower, LA Naturite	Milan, Italy	Mar. 10, 1982

Relay Events

Event	Time	Team	Location	Date
640y	1:08.99	Tennessee State U. (Chandra Cheeseborough, Ernestine Davis, Judy Pollion, Sherrell Pernel)	New York, NY	Feb. 27, 1981
800m/880y	1:36.8 p	Morgan State U. (Janet Dodson, Wilmetta Page, Roberta Belle, Nellie Bullock)	Allston, MA	Mar. 7, 1981
1600m	3:37.88	U. of Texas, (Tammy Etienne, Julie Holmes Lewis, Donna Sherfield, Robbin Coleman)	Pocatello, ID	Mar. 14, 1981

1 Mile	3:40.6	Los Angeles Mercurettes	New York, NY	Feb. 27, 1981
		(Deann Gutowski, Paulette Clagon,		
		Cindy Cumbess, Brenda Peterson)		
880y mdly	1:42.17	Tennessee State U.	New York, NY	Feb. 27, 1981
		(Ernestine Davis, Judy Pollion,		
		Sherrell Pernell, Chandra		
		Cheeseborough)		

Field Events

High Jump	2.00m (6'6¾")	Coleen Sommer, Wilt's A.C.	Ottawa, Canada	Feb. 14, 1982
Long Jump	6.52m (21'4¾")	Martha Watson, USA	Richmond, VA	Mar. 16, 1973
	6.52m p	Martha Watson, Lakewood, Int'l.	Los Angeles, CA	Jan. 16, 1976
	6.52m p	Kathy McMillan, Hoke Co. H.S.	Greensboro, NC	Feb. 19, 1976
Shot Put	18.65m (61'2¼")	Maren Seidler, San Jose Stars	Sindelfingen, GFR	Jan. 20, 1978

Indoor All-comers Records

50y	5.87 p	Evelyn Ashford, Medalist T.C.	Rosemont, IL	Jan. 17, 1982
50m	6.20 p	Evelyn Ashford, Medalist T.C.	Daly City, CA	Feb. 20, 1982
60m	7.24 p	Merlene Ottey, Nebraska	Pocatello, ID	Mar. 14, 1982
300y	32.65	Merlene Ottey, Nebraska	Cedar Falls, IA	Mar. 13, 1982
300m	35.83	Merlene Ottey, Nebraska	Pocatello, ID	Mar. 14, 1982
400m	52.88	June Griffith, Stanford T.C.	New York, NY	Feb. 12, 1982
500y	1:03.3	Janine MacGregor, England	Inglewood, CA	Feb. 5, 1982
800m R	1:36.5 p	Tennessee State U.	Louisville, KY	Feb. 9, 1979
		(Brenda Morehead, Deborah Jones,		
		Ernestine Davis, Chandra		
		Cheeseborough)		
1600m R	3:37.28	Adelphi U. (Marva Fearon,	Pocatello, ID	Mar. 14, 1981
		Cheryl Innis, Marilyn Gillard,		
		June Griffith)		
High Jump	1.96m (6'5")	Debbie Brill, Pacific Coast	Los Angeles, CA	Jan. 22, 1982
Long Jump	6.54m (21'5½")	Tatyana Schelkanova, USSR	New York, NY	Feb. 18, 1966
Shot Put	19.28m (63'3½")	Nadyezhda Chizhova, USSR	Richmond, VA	Mar. 16, 1973

Appendices

RECOMMENDED SCHEDULES OF EVENTS

The order of events and the time between events are <u>recommended and</u> <u>may be changed by the Games Committee or by mutual consent of</u> <u>teams</u>. The time of day for commencement of the schedule of event is relative to the specific situation.

One-Day Outdoor Schedule (Without Trials)

Running Events[1]	*Field Events*
0:00 5000m run	−2:00 Long Jump
+0:30 4 × 100m relay	−2:00 Shot Put
+0:40 1500m run	−2:00 Javelin
+1:00 100m hurdles	−1:00 High Jump
+1:10 400m dash	−1:00 Discus
+1:20 100m dash	
+1:30 800m run	
+1:45 400m hurdles	
+1:55 200m dash	
+2:05 3000m run	
+2:30 4 × 400m relay	

---

[1] If trials are required in certain running events, follow the order of events of the morning of the 2-day schedule.

In a one-day schedule teams seldom are able to run all the championship events. Some substitutions are suggested: the 10,000 may be either changed with the 5000 or the 3000 if so desired; the 4 × 800 meter relay may be run in place of the 800 meter race; the 800 meter medley relay may be run in place of the 4 × 400 meter relay.

One-Day Outdoor Schedule
(With Trials)

Running Events[2]

0:00	4 × 100m relay	Trials
+0:10	5000 m	Finals
+0:35	400m dash	Trials
+0:50	100m hurdles	Trials
+1:10	100m dash	Trials
+1:25	1500m run	Finals
+1:35	400m hurdles	Trials
+1:45	100m dash	Finals
+1:55	100m hurdles	Finals
+2:05	200m dash	Trials
+2:20	400m dash	Finals
+2:30	800m run	Finals
+2:40	200m dash	Finals
+2:50	400m hurdles	Finals
+3:00	3000m run	Finals
+3:15	4 × 400m relay	Finals

Field Events

−2:00	Long Jump	
−2:00	Shot Put	
−2:00	Javelin	
−1:00	High Jump	
−1:00	Discus	
−2:00	Shot Put	Prelims & Finals
−2:00	Long Jump	Prelims & Finals

---

[2]If trials are required in the running events, follow the order of events of the morning of the 2-day Indoor Schedule.

In a one-day schedule, teams seldom are able to run all the championship events. Some substitutions are suggested: the 10,000 may be either changed with the 5000 or the 3000 if so desired; the 4 × 800 meter relay may be run in place of the 800 meter race; the 800 meter medley relay may be run in place of the 4 × 400 meter relay.

Two-Day Outdoor Schedule
(With Trials)

Friday

12:30	10,000m Run
1:00	Discus (Trials & Finals
	Long Jump (Trials & Finals)
1:20	440 Relay Semis
1:40	100m Hurdle Heptathlon (1)
1:50	100m Hurdle Trials
2:10	100m Dash Trials
2:20	High Jump Heptathlon (3)
2:30	800m Run Semis
2:50	200m Dash Trials
3:10	100m Hurdles Semis
3:45	Shot Put Heptathlon (2)
3:25	400m Dash Semis
3:45	100m Dash Semis
3:55	4 × 880 Relay Finals
4:20	200m Dash Semis
4:35	400m Hurdles Semis
4:50	3000m Run Finals
5:05	200m Dash Heptathlon (4)
*5:25	880 Medley Relay Finals

Saturday

11:00	Javelin (Trials & Finals)
	Long Jump Heptathlon (5)
12:00	440 Relay Finals
	Shot Put (Trials & Finals)
12:15	1500m Run Finals

12:30	100m Hurdles Finals
	High Jump
12:45	400m Dash Finals
12:55	100m Dash Finals
1:00	Javelin Heptathlon (6)
1:10	400m Hurdles Finals
1:25	800m Run Finals
1:40	200m Dash Finals
1:50	5000m Run Finals
2:15	800m Run Heptathlon (7)
2:25	Mile Relay Finals

Two-Day Indoor Schedule
With Pentathlon

Session 1	*Session 2*
60 H (pent.), L.J. (T&F)	Distance Medley, High Jump, Shot
60 H (S)	60 H (F)
60 (S)	60 (F)
1000 (F)	1500 (F)
Shot Put-Pent.	400 (F)
4 × 1 lap Relay (F)	300 (F)
600 (F)	800 (F)
300 (T)	5000 (F)
3000 (F) HJ-Pent.	4 × 400 Relay
4 × 800 Relay (F)	
LJ-Pent.	
800-Pent.	

Dual or Triangular Indoor Meets
(One Session)

Option 1

Events—60, 300, 600, 1000, 3000, LJ, HJ, SP 4 × 1 lap relay, 4 × 800 relay

Option 2

Events—60, 300, 400, 800, 1500, 5000, 60, H, LJ, HJ, SP, 4 × 400 relay, Distance medley relay.

Order of Events

60 H, LJ, SP
60
1000
4 × 1 lap relay
600, HJ
300
3000
4 × 800 relay

Order of Events

Distance Medley, LJ, SP
60 H
60
1500
400
300
800, HJ
4 × 400 relay

One-Day Schedule (Without Trials)
For Secondary School

0:00	4 × 800m relay
0:15	100m hurdles
0:20	100m dash
0:35	1500m run
0:45	4 × 200m relay
1:00	400m dash
1:15	400m relay
1:30	200, 300, or 400m hurdles
1:50	800m run
2:00	200m dash
2:10	3000m run
2:30	800m medley relay (100-100-200-400)
2:50	4 × 400m relay
0:00	Long jump, shot put
0:30	High jump
0:45	Discus
1:30	Javelin

TRANSLATION METHODS (METRIC SYSTEM)

100y to 100m—multiply by 1.09 (or add .9 seconds)
220y to 200m—multiply by .995 (or subtract .1 seconds)
440y to 400m—multiply by .994 (or subtract .3 seconds)
880y to 800m—multiply by .9935 (or subtract .8 seconds)
Mile to 1500m—multiply by .926 (or subtract 20 seconds, very crude)
2 Mile to 3000m—multiply by .926 (or subtract 45 seconds, very crude)
100m to 100y—multiply by .9173211 (or subtract .9 seconds)
200m to 220y—multiply by 1.005 (or add .1 seconds)
400m to 440y—multiply by 1.006 (or add .3 seconds)
800m to 880y—multiply by 1.0065 (or add .8 seconds)
1500m to mile—multiply by 1.08 (or add 20 seconds, very crude)
3000m to 2 mile—multiply by 1.08 (or add 45 seconds, very crude)

From meters to feet—multiply by 3.2808
From feet to meters—multiply by .3048
100 meters = 110 yards minus 1'11" or 100 yards plus 28'1"
200 meters = 220 yards minus 3'10"
300 meters = 330 yards minus 5'9"
400 meters = 440 yards minus 7'8"
hurdles—30" = 76 cm.
    33" = 84 cm.

INTRODUCTION AND EXPLANATION OF THE ALLEY PRINCIPLE

In case the number of entries exceeds the number that would be required to advance a minimum of two to the succeeding round, alleys should be used. An "alley" is the use of two or three lanes as a single lane for the running of the first turn. For example, up to four competitors could be assembled in lanes 1 and 2 behind the extend-starting line of lane 1; another three or four competitors could be assembled in lanes 3 and 4 behind the one-turn stagger starting line of lane 3; another set of three or four runners could be assembled in lanes 5 and 6 behind the one-turn stagger starting line of lane 5; and three or four more runners using lanes 7 and 8 could be assembled behind the starting line of the seventh lane one-turn stagger.

Runners in the alleys use the inside border of their starting lane to run around the turn before breaking the curb. For example, runners in lanes 5 and 6 would use the inside border of lane five when running the first turn. All runners may break for the curb at the flag after completing the turn.

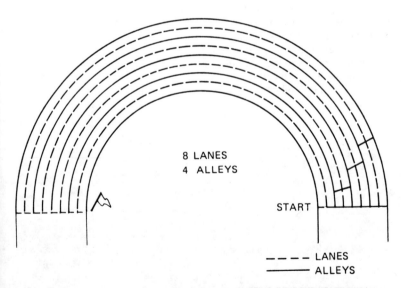

8 LANES
4 ALLEYS

START

- - - - LANES
———— ALLEYS

GLOSSARY

Acceleration zone—An area the width of one lane, 10 meters (11 yards) long which may be used by a relay runner to begin running before she receives the baton in the exchange zone.

Alley—May consist of 2–3 lanes which are used as a single lane for running the 800-meter run or 3200-meter relay from a one-turn stagger when more runners are competing than the number of lanes available.

Approach—The run used by the competitor prior to the actual take-off in the jumps and javelin, basketball and softball throws.

Apron—The hard-surfaced area in front of the high jump pit.

Break—Leaving the starting blocks or starting line before the gun sounds or making a movement from the set position.

Break in the pit—The mark made by the competitor when landing in the pit in the horizontal jumps.

Breaking for the pole—Cutting over to the inside lane of the track.

Course—A general term used to indicate the path of a runner.

Crossbar—The bar over which the high jumpers jump.

Curb—Inside border of the track.

Curved starting line—An involuted (waterfall) starting line used in 1500, 3000, 5000, and 10,000-meter races. (See Appendix B.)

Dead heat—A race in which two or more runners cross the finish line at exactly the same moment.

Exchange zone—An area the width of one lane and 20 meters (22 yards) long used in relay races. The baton must be passed from one runner to her teammate while they are in this zone. (See Passing zone.)

False start—Leaving the starting block or starting line before the gun sounds or making a movement from the set position. (See Break.)

Finish line—A line drawn on the track, the side nearest the runner marking the legal completion of the distance raced.

Finish posts—Posts on each side of the finish line to which the finish tape or string is attached.

Finish yarn or tape—The cord stretched across the track directly above the finish line to aid the finish judges in determining the winner of a race.

Flight—The breaking down of a large field of competitors into smaller competitive groups. Used in the horizontal jumps and the throwing events in order that competitors may warm up and compete within a reasonable time. Also can refer to a lane or row of hurdles.

Foul jump or throw—A jump or throw which is counted as a trial but which is not measured because of some violation of the field event rules.

Fully automatic timing—(See Rule 5, Sect. 3W.)

Grip—The handhold on a baton, discus, shot or javelin, or specifically the cord wrapping on the middle of the javelin.

Heat—A preliminary round of a race from which the designated places advance to the next round.

High jump standards—Uprights which are used to hold the crossbar for the high jump.

IAAF—International Amateur Athletic Federation.

International zone—(See Acceleration zone.)

Involuted starting line—(See Curved starting line.)

Jostle—To run against or to elbow. It is a form of crowding or bumping together which may hamper or impede a runner.

Kelly pool balls—Small numbered balls used in drawing for lanes. Also called shake balls.

Lane—The path which is marked on the track for a race, or that part of a race during which a runner must stay in a prescribed path.

Lap—One complete circuit of the entire track.

Leg of a relay—The distance over which one member of a relay team must run.

Medley relay—A relay race in which the members of the relay team run different distances.

Pass—The voluntary giving up of one of a competitor's preliminary or final jumps or throws. Also refers to the actual exchange of a baton or the overtaking of one runner by another in a race.

Passing zone—A zone the width of one lane 20 meters (22 yards) long used in relay races. The baton must be passed from a runner to her teammate while they are in this zone. (See Exchange zone.)

Pole—The inside or curb lane of the track.

Preliminaries—In running events, they are a series of heats in the same event used when there are more competitors than there are lanes. (See heat.) In the throws and long jump, preliminaries consist of three trials per competitor. The best competitors then advance to the finals for three more trials.

Qualifying round—Competition where performances qualify the athlete for positions in the trials but whose time or distances are not considered for final placing. Marks can be considered for record purposes.

Recall—The calling back of runners after a false start.

Revolving flights—See PTO, Sect. 7, 2t.

Runway—See Approach.

Scratch—Decision not to compete in an event after confirmation or declaration.

Scratch line—The curved or straight line behind which the throw must be made in the javelin and/or softball throws.

Section—Heats, the composition of which are determined by the previous best times of runners on relay teams. Usually run as finals against time with the fastest section being run last.

Sector lines—Boundary lines within which a throw must land in order to be a fair throw.

Shuttle relay—A relay run on a straightaway, with half of each relay team at opposite ends of the prescribed distance. Alternate runners run back and forth over the same course.

Staggered start—The start of a race in which runners do not start on a straight line. Used in races which are run around a curve up to and including 800 meters (880 yards).

Starting block—An implement against which runners may place their feet in order to get a faster start at the beginning of a race.

Straightaway—Straight area of the track between one curve and the next.

Stride—The distance covered by one step.

TAC—The Athletics Congress. National sports governing body for athletics, (Track & Field, Long-Distance Running, Race Walking, Youth Athletics and Masters Competition).

Tagging—Touching a relay runner instead of giving her a baton; usually used in the shuttle relays.

Take-off board—A board from which a long jumper makes her jumps.

Take-off mark—A spot at which a competitor leaves the ground, as in the high jump and long jump.

Toeboard—A curved piece of wood or metal used as a foul line for the throws.

Torso—That part of the body as distinguished from the head, neck, arms, legs, hands or feet.

Trail leg—Take-off leg or the rear leg in hurdling.

Trial—An attempt in a field event.

Turn—Curved portion of the track. A standard 400-meter (440-yard) track has two turns or curves in one lap.

USCSC—United States Collegiate Sports Council.

USOC—United States Olympic Committee.

USTFF—United States Track and Field Federation.

Visual exchange—A baton exchange in which the receiver watches the incoming runner until the pass is completed.

Warm-up—Preparation of the body through light exercise for more vigorous exercise.

Waterfall starting line—(See Curved starting line.)

APPLICATION FOR NAGWS RECORD

To NAGWS High School _____
                Junior College _____
                Collegiate _____

To **THE RECORD COMMITTEE:**

Application is hereby made for a record in support of which the following information is submitted:

Description of Record: World _____ American _____ NAGWS: High School _____ Junior College _____Collegiate _____

1. Event _____

2. Date _____ Women

3. Record claimed (state time, distance, height or points achieved) Outdoor

_____

4. Where held (Ground, Town and Country) _____

5. Condition of track, runway or circle _____ surface.

6. Level or gradient of track, runway or circle _____ (Important—See Rules)

7. Weight, measurement and materials of implements (Detail) _____

_____

8. Signature of Measurer or Weigher _____

9. Force of following wind _____Anemometer Attendant's Signature

10. Name of Competitor _____
                       (Surname)   (Christian   name)   (print)

      High School _____

      Junior College _____

      College _____
      (In relay events, the full names of the competitors should be printed)

11. If electronic timing device used, indicate type: _____

TIMEKEEPERS' CERTIFICATES

12. I, the undersigned official time keeper, of the event above-mentioned, so hereby certify that the time set opposite my signature was the exact time recorded by my watch, and that the watch used by me has been approved by the meet director according to NAGWS Track & Field Rules.

Time _____   _____   _____
                          (Signature of Timekeeper)   (Address)

Time _____   _____   _____
                          (Signature of Timekeeper)   (Address)

Time _____   _____   _____
                          (Signature of Timekeeper)   (Address)

I confirm that the above Timekeepers exhibited their watches to me and that the times as stated are correct.

_____
(Signature of Referee or Chief Timekeeper)

STARTER'S CERTIFICATE

13. I hereby certify that I was the starter for the event abovementioned, that it was a fair start and no advantage was given to or taken by the claimant.
(Refer to Rules)

_____   _____
        (Signature of Starter)   (Address)

A newspaper clipping, copy of entry blank and marked program should be attached and made part of the application.

14. Measurers' Certificate for Track and Field Events (a or b)

_____   _____
      (Signature of Measurer)   (Address)

_____   _____
      (Signature of Measurer)   (Address)

a. The *above* certify that we measured, with a metric steel tape, the course over which the above event was held and that the exact distance was:

_____ metres _____ centimetres, *or* _____ miles _____ yards

_____ feet _____ inches

The length of one lap was ____ metres ____ centimeters *or* _____ yards

____ feet ____ inches, that there was a 2 inch raised border on the inner edge of track, and that the maximum allowance for lateral inclination did not exceed 1:100 and the running direction 1:1000.

Please state if the race was on a straight course, or with one or two bends.
Cite Number of Bends (turns)
For hurdle event state number, distance, height, etc.

_____

b. Field Events

The *above* certify that the lateral inclination of the runway or circle did not exceed 1:100 and in the running direction 1:1000. (Refer to Rules, in case of world record.) Please state the degrees in the throwing events section for the H.S. application   degrees _____

JUDGES' CERTIFICATE (FIELD OR TRACK)

15. We hereby certify that the measurement stated opposite our respective signatures is exact as measured with a metric steel tape. *(Judges and Referee shall read measurement.)*

We also certify that the conditions of the ground gave no advantage to the competitor, and that the implements used and circle or runway complied with the specifications as laid down in Rules of IAAF, and were issued by the organizers. (Use for track events including racewalking on track and field events.)

We hereby certify that conditions met all NAGWS requirements.

(Distance or Height)	(Signature of Judge)	(Address)
(Distance or Height)	(Signature of Judge)	(Address)
(Distance or Height)	(Signature of Judge)	(Address)

16. I hereby certify that the Officials, Track and Field conditions, Hurdles, and Implements used were in strict accordance with existing rules of the NAGWS. _____

(Signature of Referee)   (Address)

SCORING TABLES

COMPARABLE MARKS (ACCORDING TO SCORING TABLES), QUICK SCORE CHART, AND METRIC TO FEET-INCHES TRANSLATION TABLES:

Approx. Point	50mH	60mH	100H	SP	SP(m)	HJ	HJ(m)	LJ	LJ(m)	800m
1100	6.3	7.6	12.4	62'1"	18.92	6'1½"	1.87	22'8"	6.91	1:59.1
1075	6.4	7.5	12.6	60'5¼"	18.42	6'½"	1.84	22'3¼"	6.79	2:00.6
1050	6.5	7.8	12.7	58'9½"	17.92	5'11½"	1.82	21'10½"	6.67	2:02.1
1025	6.5	7.9	12.9	57'2¼"	17.43	5'10½"	1.79	21'6"	6.55	2:03.6
1000	6.6	8.0	13.1	55'7¼"	16.95	5'9¼"	1.76	21'1¼"	6.43	2:05.1
975	6.7	8.1	13.2	54'½"	16.47	5'8½"	1.74	20'8½"	6.31	2:06.7
950	6.8	8.2	13.4	52'6¼"	16.01	5'7¼"	1.71	20'4"	6.20	2:08.4
925	6.9	8.3	13.6	51'	15.54	5'6½"	1.69	19'11½"	6.07	2:10.1
900	7.0	8.4	13.8	49'6"	15.09	5'5½"	1.66	19'7"	5.97	2:11.8
875	7.1	8.5	14.0	48'½"	14.64	5'4½"	1.64	19'2½"	5.86	2:13.6
850	7.2	8.6	14.2	46'7"	14.20	5'3½"	1.61	18'10"	5.74	2:15.4
825	7.3	8.7	14.4	45'2"	13.76	5'2½"	1.59	18'5½"	5.63	2:17.3
800	7.4	8.9	14.6	43'9¼"	13.34	5'1½"	1.56	18'1¼"	5.52	2:19.2
775	7.5	9.0	14.8	42'5"	12.93	5'½"	1.54	17'9"	5.41	2:21.2
750	7.6	9.1	15.0	41'¼"	12.50	4'11½"	1.51	17'5"	5.31	2:23.2
725	7.7	9.3	15.3	39'8"	12.09	4'10½"	1.49	17'½"	5.20	2:25.3
700	7.9	9.4	15.5	38'4¼"	11.69	4'10"	1.47	16'8½"	5.09	2:27.5
675	8.0	9.6	15.7	37'1"	11.30	4'9"	1.45	16'4½"	4.99	2:29.7
650	8.1	9.7	16.0	35'9½"	10.91	4'8¼"	1.43	16'½"	4.89	2:32.0
625	8.2	9.9	16.3	34'6½"	10.53	4'7½"	1.41	15'8¼"	4.78	2:34.4
600	8.4	10.0	16.5	33'4"	10.16	4'6½"	1.39	15'4¼"	4.68	2:36.9
575	8.5	10.2	16.8	32'1½"	9.79	4'5½"	1.36	15'¼"	4.58	2:39.4
550	8.7	10.4	17.1	30'11¼"	9.43	4'4½"	1.34	14'8½"	4.48	2:42.0
525	8.9	10.6	17.4	29'9½"	9.08	4'4"	1.32	14'4½"	4.38	2:44.7
500	9.0	10.8	17.7	28'8"	8.74	4'3¼"	1.30	14'1"	4.29	2:47.5
475	9.2	11.0	18.1	27'6¼"	8.39	4'2½"	1.28	13'9"	4 19	2:50.4
450	9.3	11.2	18.4	26'5"	8.05	4'2"	1.27	13'5½"	4.10	2:53.4
425	9.5	11.4	18.7	25'4¼"	7.73	4'1¼"	1.25	13'2"	4.01	2:56.5
400	9.7	11.6	19.1	24'4"	7.41	4'½"	1.23	12'10"	3.91	2:59.7
375	9.9	11.8	19.5	23'3½"	7.10	3'11½"	1.21	12'6½"	3.82	3:03.0
350	10.1	12.1	19.9	22'3¼"	6.79	3'11"	1.19	12'3"	3.73	3:06.4
325	10.3	12.3	20.3	21'3½"	6.49	3'10½"	1.18	11'11¼"	3.64	3:10.0
300	10.5	12.6	20.7	20'4"	6.20	3'9½"	1.16	11'7½"	3.54	3:13.7
275	10.7	12.8	21.1	19'5"	5.92	3'9"	1.14	11'4½"	3.46	3:17.6
250	11.0	13.1	21.6	18'6"	5.64	3'8½"	1.13	11'1"	3.38	3:21.6
225	11.2	13.4	22.1	17'7"	5.36	3'7½"	1.11	10'9½"	3.29	3:25.8
200	11.5	13.7	22.6	16'8½"	5.09	3'7"	1.09	10'6½"	3.21	3:30.2
175	11.7	14.0	23.1	15'10¼"	4.83	3'6½"	1.08	10'3¼"	3.13	3:34.8
150	12.0	14.3	23.6	15'¼"	4.58	3'5½"	1.06	10'	3.05	3:39.6
125	12.3	14.7	24.2	14'3"	4.34	3'5¼"	1.05	9'9"	2.97	3:44.5
100	12.6	15.1	24.8	13'5½"	4.10	3'5"	1.04	9'5½"	2.88	3:49.8
75	13.0	15.5	25.4	12'8"	3.86	3'4¼"	1.02	9'2½"	2.80	3:55.2
50	13.3	15.9	26.1	11'11¼"	3.64	3'3½"	1.00	8'11½"	2.73	4:01.0
25	13.7	16.4	26.8	11'3"	3.43			8'8¼"	2.65	4:07.0
0	14.2	16.9	27.6	10'6"	3.20			8'6"	2.59	4:13.1

Pentathlon—Triathlon—Heptathlon
Scoring Tables

50 METER HURDLES (4 HURDLES):

Time	Points	Time	Points	Time	Points	Time	Points
6.2	1129	8.3	615	10.4	314	12.5	108
6.3	1097	8.4	597	10.5	302	12.6	100
6.4	1066	8.5	580	10.6	290	12.7	93
6.5	1035	8.6	563	10.7	279	12.8	86
6.6	1005	8.7	547	10.8	268	12.9	79
6.7	976	8.8	531	10.9	257	13.0	72
6.8	948	8.9	515	11.0	246	13.1	65
6.9	921	9.0	500	11.1	236	13.2	58
7.0	895	9.1	485	11.2	226	13.3	51
7.1	870	9.2	470	11.3	216	13.4	44
7.2	846	9.3	456	11.4	206	13.5	37
7.3	822	9.4	442	11.5	196	13.6	31
7.4	799	9.5	428	11.6	187	13.7	25
7.5	776	9.6	415	11.7	178	13.8	19
7.6	754	9.7	402	11.8	169	13.9	13
7.7	732	9.8	389	11.9	160	14.0	8
7.8	711	9.9	376	12.0	151	14.1	3
7.9	691	10.0	363	12.1	142	14.2	0
8.0	671	10.1	350	12.2	133		
8.1	652	10.2	338	12.3	124		
8.2	633	10.3	326	12.4	116		

60 METER HURDLES (5 HURDLES):

Time	Points	Time	Points	Time	Points	Time	Points
7.5	1121	9.9	622	12.3	327	14.7	125
7.6	1093	10.0	607	12.4	317	14.8	118
7.7	1066	10.1	592	12.5	307	14.9	111
7.8	1040	10.2	577	12.6	297	15.0	104
7.9	1015	10.3	563	12.7	287	15.1	97
8.0	991	10.4	549	12.8	277	15.2	90
8.1	967	10.5	535	12.9	268	15.3	84
8.2	944	10.6	522	13.0	259	15.4	78
8.3	921	10.7	509	13.1	250	15.5	72
8.4	899	10.8	496	13.2	241	15.6	66
8.5	877	10.9	483	13.3	232	15.7	60
8.6	856	11.0	471	13.4	223	15.8	54
8.7	835	11.1	459	13.5	215	15.9	48
8.8	815	11.2	447	13.6	207	16.0	43
8.9	795	11.3	435	13.7	199	16.1	38
9.0	776	11.4	424	13.8	191	16.2	33
9.1	757	11.5	413	13.9	183	16.3	28
9.2	739	11.6	402	14.0	175	16.4	23
9.3	721	11.7	391	14.1	167	16.5	18
9.4	704	11.8	380	14.2	160	16.6	13
9.5	687	11.9	369	14.3	153	16.7	8
9.6	670	12.0	358	14.4	146	16.8	3
9.7	654	12.1	347	14.5	139	16.9	0
9.8	638	12.2	337	14.6	132		

100 METRES HURDLES*

Time	Points	Time	Points	Time	Points	Time	Points
•							
12.0	1160	16.0	645	20.0	339	24.0	132
12.1	1143	16.1	636	20.1	333	24.1	128
12.2	1126	16.2	626	20.2	327	24.2	124
12.3	1110	16.3	617	20.3	321	24.3	120
12.4	1094	16.4	608	20.4	315	24.4	115
12.5	1078	16.5	598	20.5	309	24.5	111
12.6	1062	16.6	589	20.6	303	24.6	107
12.7	1047	16.7	580	20.7	297	24.7	103
12.8	1031	16.8	572	20.8	291	24.8	99
12.9	1016	16.9	563	20.9	286	24.9	95
13.0	1002	17.0	554	21.0	280	25.0	91
13.1	987	17.1	546	21.1	274	25.1	87
13.2	973	17.2	537	21.2	269	25.2	83
13.3	959	17.3	529	21.3	263	25.3	79
13.4	945	17.4	521	21.4	258	25.4	75
13.5	931	17.5	513	21.5	252	25.5	72
13.6	918	17.6	505	21.6	247	25.6	68
13.7	905	17.7	499	21.7	242	25.7	64
13.8	891	17.8	493	21.8	237	25.8	60
13.9	879	17.9	485	21.9	231	25.9	57
14.0	866	18.0	477	22.0	226	26.0	53
14.1	853	18.1	469	22.1	221	26.1	49
14.2	841	18.2	462	22.2	216	26.2	46
14.3	829	18.3	454	22.3	211	26.3	42
14.4	817	18.4	447	22.4	206	26.4	38
14.5	805	18.5	440	22.5	201	26.5	35
14.6	793	18.6	433	22.6	196	26.6	31
14.7	782	18.7	425	22.7	191	26.7	28
14.8	770	18.8	418	22.8	187	26.8	24
14.9	759	18.9	411	22.9	182	26.9	21
15.0	748	19.0	404	23.0	177	27.0	18
15.1	737	19.1	398	23.1	173	27.1	14
15.2	727	19.2	391	23.2	168	27.2	11
15.3	716	19.3	384	23.3	163	27.3	7
15.4	705	19.4	377	23.4	159	27.4	4
15.5	695	19.5	371	23.5	154	27.5	1
15.6	685	19.6	364	23.6	150		
15.7	675	19.7	358	23.7	145		
15.8	665	19.8	352	23.8	141	11.8	1195
15.9	655	19.9	345	23.9	137	11.9	1177

*Reprinted with permission of the International Amateur Athletic Federation. Copyright © held by the I.A.A.F.

NATIONAL ASSOCIATION FOR GIRLS & WOMEN IN SPORT

100 METRES HURDLES*

Time	Points	Time	Points	Time	Points	Time	Points	Time	Points
11.80	1195	12.30	1110	12.80	1031	13.30	959	13.80	891
81	1193	31	1108	81	1030	31	957	81	890
82	1192	32	1107	82	1028	32	956	82	889
83	1190	33	1105	83	1027	33	955	83	888
84	1188	34	1103	84	1025	34	953	84	886
85	1186	35	1102	85	1024	35	952	85	885
86	1184	36	1100	86	1022	36	950	86	884
87	1183	37	1099	87	1021	37	949	87	882
88	1181	38	1097	88	1019	38	948	88	881
89	1179	39	1095	89	1018	39	946	89	880
11.90	1177	12.40	1094	12.90	1016	13.40	945	13.90	879
91	1176	41	1092	91	1015	41	944	91	877
92	1174	42	1090	92	1013	42	942	92	876
93	1172	43	1089	93	1012	43	941	93	875
94	1170	44	1087	94	1011	44	939	94	873
95	1169	45	1086	95	1009	45	938	95	872
96	1167	46	1084	96	1008	46	937	96	871
97	1165	47	1083	97	1006	47	935	97	870
98	1164	48	1081	98	1005	48	934	98	868
99	1162	49	1079	99	1003	49	933	99	867
12.00	1160	12.50	1078	13.00	1002	13.50	931	14.00	866
01	1158	51	1076	01	1000	51	930	01	865
02	1157	52	1075	02	999	52	929	02	863
03	1155	53	1073	03	997	53	927	03	862
04	1153	54	1071	04	996	54	926	04	861
05	1152	55	1070	05	994	55	925	05	860
06	1150	56	1068	06	993	56	923	06	858
07	1148	57	1067	07	992	57	922	07	857
08	1147	58	1065	08	990	58	920	08	856
09	1145	59	1064	09	989	59	919	09	855
12.10	1143	12.60	1062	13.10	987	13.60	918	14.10	853
11	1141	61	1060	11	986	61	916	11	852
12	1140	62	1059	12	984	62	915	12	851
13	1138	63	1057	13	983	63	914	13	850
14	1136	64	1056	14	981	64	912	14	848
15	1135	65	1054	15	980	65	911	15	847
16	1133	66	1053	16	979	66	910	16	846
17	1131	67	1051	17	977	67	909	17	845
18	1130	68	1050	18	976	68	907	18	843
19	1128	69	1048	19	974	69	906	19	842
12.20	1126	12.70	1047	13.20	973	13.70	905	14.20	841
21	1125	71	1045	21	971	71	903	21	840
22	1123	72	1044	22	970	72	902	22	839
23	1121	73	1042	23	969	73	901	23	837
24	1120	74	1040	24	967	74	899	24	836
25	1118	75	1039	25	966	75	898	25	835
26	1116	76	1037	26	964	76	897	26	834
27	1115	77	1036	27	963	77	895	27	832
28	1113	78	1034	28	962	78	894	28	831
29	1112	79	1033	29	960	79	893	29	830

*Reprinted with permission of the International Amateur Athletic Federation. Copyright © held by the I.A.A.F.

100 METRES HURDLES*

Time	Points	Time	Points	Time	Points	Time	Points	Time	Points
14.30	829	14.80	770	15.30	716	15.80	665	16.30	617
31	828	81	769	31	715	81	664	31	616
32	826	82	768	32	714	82	663	32	615
33	825	83	767	33	713	83	662	33	614
34	824	84	766	34	712	84	661	34	613
35	823	85	765	35	711	85	660	35	612
36	822	86	764	36	710	86	659	36	611
37	820	87	763	37	709	87	658	37	610
38	819	88	761	38	707	88	657	38	609
39	818	89	760	39	706	89	656	39	608
14.40	817	14.90	759	15.40	705	15.90	655	16.40	608
41	816	91	758	41	704	91	654	41	607
42	814	92	757	42	703	92	653	42	606
43	813	93	756	43	702	93	652	43	605
44	812	94	755	44	701	94	651	44	604
45	811	95	754	45	700	95	650	45	603
46	810	96	753	46	699	96	649	46	602
47	809	97	751	47	698	97	648	47	601
48	807	98	750	48	697	98	647	48	600
49	806	99	749	49	696	99	646	49	599
14.50	805	15.00	748	15.50	695	16.00	645	16.50	598
51	804	01	747	51	694	01	644	51	597
52	803	02	746	52	693	02	643	52	597
53	801	03	745	53	692	03	642	53	596
54	800	04	744	54	691	04	641	54	595
55	799	05	743	55	690	05	640	55	594
56	798	06	742	56	689	06	639	56	593
57	797	07	741	57	688	07	638	57	592
58	796	08	739	58	687	08	638	58	591
59	794	09	738	59	686	09	637	59	590
14.60	793	15.10	737	15.60	685	16.10	636	16.60	589
61	792	11	736	61	684	11	635	61	588
62	791	12	735	62	683	12	634	62	588
63	790	13	734	63	682	13	633	63	587
64	789	14	733	64	681	14	632	64	586
65	788	15	732	65	680	15	631	65	585
66	786	16	731	66	679	16	630	66	584
67	785	17	730	67	678	17	629	67	583
68	784	18	729	68	677	18	628	68	582
69	783	19	728	69	676	19	627	69	581
14.70	782	15.20	727	15.70	675	16.20	626	16.70	580
71	781	21	725	71	674	21	625	71	580
72	780	22	724	72	673	22	624	72	579
73	778	23	723	73	672	23	623	73	578
74	777	24	722	74	671	24	622	74	577
75	776	25	721	75	670	25	621	75	576
76	775	26	720	76	669	26	621	76	575
77	774	27	719	77	668	27	620	77	574
78	773	28	718	78	667	28	619	78	573
79	772	29	717	79	666	29	618	79	573

To assess times slower than 16.70, use 100 metres Hurdles Table on page 00 and calculate accordingly.

*Reprinted with permission of the International Amateur Athletic Federation. Copyright © held by the I.A.A.F.

NATIONAL ASSOCIATION FOR GIRLS & WOMEN IN SPORT

HIGH JUMP

M.	Points	M.	Points	M.	Points	M.	Points
1.98	1193	1.70	935	1.42	635	1.15	279
1.97	1184	1.69	925	1.41	624	1.14	264
1.96	1175	1.68	915	1.40	612	1.13	249
1.95	1166	1.67	905	1.39	600	1.12	233
1.94	1158	1.66	895	1.38	588	1.11	217
1.93	1149	1.65	885	1.37	576	1.10	201
1.92	1140	1.64	875	1.36	564	1.09	185
1.91	1131	1.63	865	1.35	551	1.08	168
1.90	1122	1.62	854	1.34	539	1.07	152
1.89	1113	1.61	844	1.33	526	1.06	135
1.88	1104	1.60	834	1.32	514	1.05	117
1.87	1095	1.59	823	1.31	501	1.04	100
1.86	1086	1.58	813	1.30	488	1.03	82
1.85	1077	1.57	802	1.29	475	1.02	64
1.84	1068	1.56	791	1.28	462	1.01	45
1.83	1059	1.55	781	1.27	449		
1.82	1049	1.54	770	1.26	435		
1.81	1040	1.53	759	1.25	422		
1.80	1031	1.52	748	1.24	408		
1.79	1021	1.51	737	1.23	395		
1.78	1012	1.50	726	1.22	381		
1.77	1002	1.49	715	1.21	367		
1.76	993	1.48	704	1.20	353		
1.75	983	1.47	693	1.19	338		
1.74	974	1.46	682	1.18	324		
1.73	964	1.45	670	1.17	309		
1.72	954	1.44	659	1.16	294		
1.71	945	1.43	647				

LONG JUMP

M.	Points	M.	Points	M.	Points	M.	Points
7.40	1197	7.20	1158	7.00	1117	6.80	1076
7.39	1195	7.19	1156	6.99	1115	6.79	1074
7.38	1193	7.18	1154	6.98	1113	6.78	1072
7.37	1191	7.17	1152	6.97	1111	6.77	1070
7.36	1189	7.16	1150	6.96	1109	6.76	1068
7.35	1187	7.15	1147	6.95	1107	6.75	1066
7.34	1185	7.14	1145	6.94	1105	6.74	1064
7.33	1183	7.13	1143	6.93	1103	6.73	1063
7.32	1181	7.12	1141	6.92	1101	6.72	1060
7.31	1179	7.11	1139	6.91	1099	6.71	1058
7.30	1177	7.10	1137	6.90	1097	6.70	1056
7.29	1176	7.09	1135	6.89	1095	6.69	1053
7.28	1174	7.08	1133	6.88	1093	6.68	1051
7.27	1172	7.07	1131	6.87	1091	6.67	1049
7.26	1170	7.06	1129	6.86	1089	6.66	1047
7.25	1168	7.05	1127	6.85	1087	6.65	1045
7.24	1166	7.04	1125	6.84	1084	6.64	1043
7.23	1164	7.03	1123	6.83	1082	6.63	1041
7.22	1162	7.02	1121	6.82	1080	6.62	1039
7.21	1160	7.01	1119	6.81	1078	6.61	1037

LONG JUMP

M.	Points	M.	Points	M.	Points	M.	Points
6.60	1035	6.10	928	5.60	817	5.10	701
6.59	1033	6.09	926	5.59	815	5.09	698
6.58	1030	6.08	924	5.58	812	5.08	696
6.57	1028	6.07	921	5.57	810	5.07	693
6.56	1026	6.06	919	5.56	808	5.06	691
6.55	1024	6.05	917	5.55	805	5.05	689
6.54	1022	6.04	915	5.54	803	5.04	686
6.53	1020	6.03	913	5.53	801	5.03	684
6.52	1018	6.02	910	5.52	799	5.02	681
6.51	1016	6.01	908	5.51	796	5.01	679
6.50	1014	6.00	906	5.50	794	5.00	677
6.49	1012	5.99	904	5.49	792	4.99	674
6.48	1009	5.98	902	5.48	789	4.98	672
6.47	1007	5.97	900	5.47	787	4.97	669
6.46	1005	5.96	897	5.46	785	4.96	667
6.45	1003	5.95	895	5.45	782	4.95	665
6.44	1001	5.94	893	5.44	780	4.94	662
6.43	999	5.93	891	5.43	778	4.93	660
6.42	997	5.92	888	5.42	776	4.92	657
6.41	995	5.91	886	5.41	773	4.91	655
6.40	992	5.90	884	5.40	771	4.90	652
6.39	990	5.89	882	5.39	769	4.89	650
6.38	988	5.88	880	5.38	766	4.88	648
6.37	986	5.87	877	5.37	764	4.87	645
6.36	984	5.86	875	5.36	762	4.86	643
6.35	982	5.85	873	5.35	759	4.85	640
6.34	980	5.84	871	5.34	757	4.84	638
6.33	978	5.83	869	5.33	755	4.83	635
6.32	975	5.82	866	5.32	752	4.82	633
6.31	973	5.81	864	5.31	750	4.81	630
6.30	971	5.80	862	5.30	748	4.80	628
6.29	969	5.79	860	5.29	745	4.79	626
6.28	967	5.78	857	5.28	743	4.78	623
6.27	965	5.77	855	5.27	741	4.77	621
6.26	963	5.76	853	5.26	738	4.76	618
6.25	960	5.75	851	5.25	736	4.75	616
6.24	958	5.74	848	5.24	734	4.74	613
6.23	956	5.73	846	5.23	731	4.73	611
6.22	954	5.72	844	5.22	729	4.72	608
6.21	952	5.71	842	5.21	727	4.71	606
6.20	950	5.70	839	5.20	724	4.70	603
6.19	947	5.69	837	5.19	722	4.69	601
6.18	945	5.68	835	5.18	720	4.68	598
6.17	943	5.67	833	5.17	717	4.67	596
6.16	941	5.66	830	5.16	715	4.66	593
6.15	939	5.65	828	5.15	712	4.65	591
6.14	937	5.64	826	5.14	710	4.64	588
6.13	934	5.63	824	5.13	708	4.63	586
6.12	932	5.62	821	5.12	705	4.62	583
6.11	930	5.61	819	5.11	703	4.61	581

NATIONAL ASSOCIATION FOR GIRLS & WOMEN IN SPORT

LONG JUMP

M.	Points	M.	Points	M	Points	M.	Points
4.60	578	4.10	449	3.60	312	3.10	166
4.59	576	4.09	447	3.59	310	3.09	162
4.58	573	4.08	444	3.58	307	3.08	159
4.57	571	4.07	442	3.57	304	3.07	156
4.56	568	4.06	439	3.56	301	3.06	153
4.55	566	4.05	436	3.55	298	3.05	150
4.54	563	4.04	434	3.54	295	3.04	147
4.53	561	4.03	331	3.53	293	3.03	144
4.52	558	4.02	428	3.52	290	3.02	141
4.51	556	4.01	425	3.51	287	3.01	138
4.50	553	4.00	423	3.50	284	3.00	135
4.49	551	3.99	420	3.49	281	2.99	132
4.48	548	3.98	417	3.48	278	2.98	129
4.47	546	3.97	415	3.47	275	2.97	125
4.46	543	3.96	412	3.46	272	2.96	122
4.45	541	3.95	409	3.45	269	2.95	119
4.44	538	3.94	407	3.44	267	2.94	116
4.43	535	3.93	404	3.43	264	2.93	113
4.42	533	3.92	401	3.42	261	2.92	110
4.41	530	3.91	398	3.41	258	2.91	107
4.40	528	3.90	396	3.40	255	2.90	103
4.39	525	3.89	393	3.39	252	2.89	100
4.38	523	3.88	390	3.38	249	2.88	97
4.37	520	3.87	388	3.37	246	2.87	94
4.36	517	3.86	385	3.36	243	2.86	91
4.35	515	3.85	382	3.35	240	2.85	88
4.34	512	3.84	379	3.34	237	2.84	84
4.33	510	3.83	377	3.33	234	2.83	81
4.32	507	3.82	374	3.32	232	2.82	78
4.31	505	3.81	371	3.31	229	2.81	75
4.30	502	3.80	368	3.30	226	2.80	72
4.29	499	3.79	366	3.29	223	2.79	68
4.28	497	3.78	363	3.28	220	2.78	65
4.27	494	3.77	360	3.27	217	2.77	62
4.26	492	3.76	357	3.26	214	2.76	59
4.25	489	3.75	355	3.25	211	2.75	55
4.24	486	3.74	352	3.24	208	2.74	52
4.23	484	3.73	349	3.23	205	2.73	49
4.22	481	3.72	346	3.22	202	2.72	46
4.21	479	3.71	343	3.21	199	2.71	42
4.20	476	3.70	341	3.20	196	2.70	39
4.19	473	3.69	338	3.19	193	2.69	36
4.18	471	3.68	335	3.18	190	2.68	33
4.17	468	3.67	332	3.17	187	2.67	29
4.16	465	3.66	329	3.16	184	2.66	26
4.15	463	3.65	327	3.15	181	2.65	23
4.14	460	3.64	324	3.14	178	2.64	19
4.13	457	3.63	321	3.13	175	2.63	16
4.12	455	3.62	318	3.12	172	2.62	13
4.11	452	3.61	315	3.11	169	2.61	10
						2.60	6

SHOT PUT, JAVELIN, 200 M, AND 800 M COMBINED TABLES

Points	Shot Put M	Javelin M	200 M Secs.	800 M Mins.	Shot Put M	Javelin M	200 M Secs.	800 M Mins.	Points
1200	21.00	72.56	—	1:53.6	19.86	67.98	—	1:56.5	1146
1199	20.97	72.48	—	1:53.7	19.84	67.90	22.0	—	1145
1198	20.95	72.40	—	—	19.82	67.82	—	1:56.6	1144
1197	20.93	72.30	—	1:53.8	19.80	67.74	—	1:56.7	1143
1196	20.91	72.22	—	—	19.78	67.64	—	—	1142
1195	20.89	72.14	—	1:53.9	19.76	67.56	—	1:56.8	1141
1194	20.87	72.04	—	—	19.74	67.48	—	—	1140
1193	20.85	71.96	—	1:54.0	19.72	67.40	—	1:56.9	1139
1192	20.83	71.88	—	—	19.70	67.32	—	—	1138
1191	20.80	71.78	21.6	1:54.1	19.67	67.24	—	1:57.0	1137
1190	20.78	71.70	—	—	19.65	67.16	—	—	1136
1189	20.76	71.62	—	1:54.2	19.63	67.06	—	1:57.1	1135
1188	20.74	71.54	—	—	19.61	66.98	22.1	1:57.2	1134
1187	20.72	71.44	—	1:54.3	19.59	66.90	—	—	1133
1186	20.70	71.36	—	—	19.57	66.82	—	1:57.3	1132
1185	20.68	71.28	—	1:54.4	19.55	66.74	—	—	1131
1184	20.66	71.20	—	—	19.53	66.66	—	1:57.4	1130
1183	20.64	71.10	—	1:54.5	19.51	66.58	—	—	1129
1182	20.61	71.02	—	—	19.49	66.48	—	1:57.5	1128
1181	20.59	70.94	—	1:54.6	19.47	66.40	—	—	1127
1180	20.57	70.84	—	1:54.7	19.45	66.32	—	1:57.6	1126
1179	20.55	70.76	21.7	—	19.43	66.24	—	1:57.7	1125
1178	20.53	70.68	—	1:54.8	19.41	66.16	—	—	1124
1177	20.51	70.60	—	—	19.39	66.08	—	1:57.8	1123
1176	20.49	70.50	—	1:54.9	19.37	66.00	22.2	—	1122
1175	20.47	70.42	—	—	19.35	65.92	—	1:57.9	1121
1174	20.45	70.34	—	1:55.0	19.33	65.84	—	—	1120
1173	20.42	70.26	—	—	19.31	65.74	—	1:58.0	1119
1172	20.40	70.16	—	1:55.1	19.28	65.66	—	—	1118
1171	20.38	70.08	—	—	19.26	65.58	—	1:58.1	1117
1170	20.36	70.00	—	1:55.2	19.24	65.50	—	1:58.2	1116
1169	20.34	69.92	—	—	19.22	65.42	—	—	1115
1168	20.32	69.84	21.8	1:55.3	19.20	65.34	—	1:58.3	1114
1167	20.30	69.74	—	1:55.4	19.18	65.26	—	—	1113
1166	20.28	69.66	—	—	19.16	65.18	—	1:58.4	1112
1165	20.26	69.58	—	1:55.5	19.14	65.10	22.3	—	1111
1164	20.24	69.50	—	—	19.12	65.02	—	1:58.5	1110
1163	20.21	69.40	—	1:55.6	19.10	64.92	—	1:58.6	1109
1162	20.19	69.32	—	—	19.08	64.84	—	—	1108
1161	20.17	69.24	—	1:55.7	19.06	64.76	—	1:58.7	1107
1160	20.15	69.16	—	—	19.04	64.68	—	—	1106
1159	20.13	69.08	—	1:55.8	19.02	64.60	—	1:58.8	1105
1158	20.11	68.98	—	—	19.00	64.52	—	—	1104
1157	20.09	68.90	—	1:55.9	18.98	64.44	—	1:58.9	1103
1156	20.07	68.82	21.9	—	18.96	64.36	—	1:59.0	1102
1155	20.05	68.74	—	1:56.0	18.94	64.28	—	—	1101
1154	20.03	68.66	—	1:56.1	18.92	64.20	22.4	1:59.1	1100
1153	20.01	68.56	—	—	18.90	64.12	—	—	1099
1152	19.99	68.48	—	1:56.2	18.88	64.04	—	1:59.2	1098
1151	19.96	68.40	—	—	18.86	63.96	—	—	1097
1150	19.94	68.32	—	1:56.3	18.84	63.88	—	1:59.3	1096
1149	19.92	68.24	—	—	18.82	63.80	—	1:59.4	1095
1148	19.90	68.14	—	1:56.4	18.80	63.72	—	—	1094
1147	19.88	68.06	—	—	18.78	63.64	—	1:59.5	1093
Points	Shot Put	Javelin	200 M	800 M	Shot Put	Javelin	200 M	800 M	Points

NATIONAL ASSOCIATION FOR GIRLS & WOMEN IN SPORT

Points	Shot Put M	Javelin M	200 M Secs.	800 M Mins.
1092	18.76	63.56	—	
1091	18.74	63.48	—	1:59.6
1090	18.72	63.38	22.5	—
1089	18.70	63.30	—	1:59.7
1088	18.68	63.22	—	1:59.8
1087	18.66	63.14	—	
1086	18.64	63.06	—	1:59.9
1085	18.62	62.98	—	
1084	18.60	62.90	—	2:00.0
1083	18.58	62.82	—	2:00.1
1082	18.56	62.74	—	—
1081	18.54	62.66	—	2:00.2
1080	18.52	62.58	—	—
1079	18.50	62.50	22.6	2:00.3
1078	18.48	62.42	—	
1077	18.46	62.34	—	2:00.4
1076	18.44	62.26	—	2:00.5
1075	18.42	62.18	—	
1074	18.40	62.10	—	2:00.6
1073	18.38	62.02	—	
1072	18.36	61.94	—	2:00.7
1071	18.34	61.86	—	2:00.8
1070	18.32	61.78	—	
1069	18.30	61.70	—	2:00.9
1068	18.28	61.62	22.7	
1067	18.26	61.54	—	2:01.0
1066	18.24	61.48	—	2:01.1
1065	18.22	61.40	—	
1064	18.20	61.32	—	2:01.2
1063	18.18	61.24	—	
1062	18.16	61.16	—	2:01.3
1061	18.14	61.08	—	2:01.4
1060	18.12	61.00	—	
1059	18.10	60.92	—	2:01.5
1058	18.08	60.84	22.8	
1057	18.06	60.76	—	2:01.6
1056	18.04	60.68	—	2:01.7
1055	18.02	60.60	—	
1054	18.00	60.52	—	2:01.8
1053	17.98	60.44	—	
1052	17.96	60.36	—	2:01.9
1051	17.94	60.28	—	2:02.0
1050	17.92	60.20	—	
1049	17.90	60.12	—	2:02.1
1048	17.88	60.06	—	
1047	17.86	59.98	22.9	2:02.2
1046	17.84	59.90	—	2:02.3
1045	17.82	59.82	—	
1044	17.80	59.74	—	2:02.4
1043	17.78	59.66	—	
1042	17.76	59.58	—	2:02.5
1041	17.74	59.50	—	2:02.6

Shot Put M	Javelin M	200 M Secs.	800 M Mins.	Points
17.72	59.42	—		1040
17.70	59.34	—	2:02.7	1039
17.69	59.26	—	—	1038
17.67	59.20	23.0	2:02.8	1037
17.65	59.12	—	2:02.9	1036
17.63	59.04	—	—	1035
17.61	58.96	—	2:03.0	1034
17.59	58.88	—	—	1033
17.57	58.80	—	2:03.1	1032
17.55	58.72	—	2:03.2	1031
17.53	58.64	—	—	1030
17.51	58.56	—	2:03.3	1029
17.49	58.50	—	2:03.4	1028
17.47	58.42	—	—	1027
17.45	58.34	23.1	2:03.5	1026
17.43	58.26	—	—	1025
17.41	58.18	—	2:03.6	1024
17.39	58.10	—	2:03.7	1023
17.37	58.02	—	—	1022
17.35	57.96	—	2:03.8	1021
17.34	57.88	—	—	1020
17.32	57.80	—	2:03.9	1019
17.30	57.72	—	2:04.0	1018
17.28	57.64	—	—	1017
17.26	57.56	23.2	2:04.1	1016
17.24	57.50	—	2:04.2	1015
17.22	57.42	—	—	1014
17.20	57.34	—	2:04.3	1013
17.18	57.26	—	—	1012
17.16	57.18	—	2:04.4	1011
17.14	57.10	—	2:04.5	1010
17.12	57.04	—	—	1009
17.10	56.96	—	2:04.6	1008
17.08	56.88	—	2:04.7	1007
17.07	56.80	23.3	—	1006
17.05	56.72	—	2:04.8	1005
17.03	56.64	—	—	1004
17.01	56.58	—	2:04.9	1003
16.99	56.50	—	2:05.0	1002
16.97	56.42	—	—	1001
16.95	56.34	—	2:05.1	1000
16.93	56.26	—	2:05.2	999
16.91	56.20	—	—	998
16.89	56.12	—	2:05.3	997
16.87	56.04	23.4	2:05.4	996
16.85	55.96	—	—	995
16.84	55.90	—	2:05.5	994
16.82	55.82	—	—	993
16.80	55.74	—	2:05.6	992
16.78	55.66	—	2:05.7	991
16.76	55.58	—	—	990
16.74	55.52	—	2:05.8	989
16.72	55.44	—	2:05.9	988

SHOT PUT, JAVELIN, 200 M, AND 800 M COMBINED TABLES

Points	Shot Put M	Javelin M	200 M Secs.	800 M Mins.	Shot Put M	Javelin M	200 M Secs.	800 M Mins.	Points
987	16.70	55.36	—	—	15.71	51.44	—	—	934
986	16.68	55.28	23.5	2:06.0	15.69	51.36	—	2:09.5	933
985	16.66	55.22	—	2:06.1	15.67	51.30	—	2:09.6	932
984	16.65	55.14	—	—	15.65	51.22	—	—	931
983	16.63	55.06	—	2:06.2	15.64	51.16	—	2:09.7	930
982	16.61	54.98	—	2:06.3	15.62	51.08	—	2:09.8	929
981	16.59	54.92	—	—	15.60	51.00	24.1	—	928
980	16.57	54.84	—	2:06.4	15.58	50.94	—	2:09.9	927
979	16.55	54.76	—	—	15.56	50.86	—	2:10.0	926
978	16.53	54.68	—	2:06.5	15.54	50.80	—	—	925
977	16.51	54.62	—	2:06.6	15.53	50.72	—	2:10.1	924
976	16.49	54.54	23.6	—	15.51	50.64	—	2:10.2	923
975	16.47	54.46	—	2:06.7	15.49	50.58	—	—	922
974	16.46	54.38	—	2:06.8	15.47	50.50	—	2:10.3	921
973	16.44	54.32	—	—	15.45	50.44	—	2:10.4	920
972	16.42	54.24	—	2:06.9	15.43	50.36	24.2	—	919
971	16.40	54.16	—	2:07.0	15.42	50.28	—	2:10.5	918
970	16.38	54.08	—	—	15.40	50.22	—	2:10.6	917
969	16.36	54.02	—	2:07.1	15.38	50.14	—	2:10.7	916
968	16.34	53.94	—	2:07.2	15.36	50.08	—	—	915
967	16.32	53.86	—	—	15.34	50.00	—	2:10.8	914
966	16.31	53.80	23.7	2:07.3	15.33	49.92	—	2:10.9	913
965	16.29	53.72	—	2:07.4	15.31	49.86	—	—	912
964	16.27	53.64	—	—	15.29	49.78	—	2:11.0	911
963	16.25	53.56	—	2:07.5	15.27	49.72	—	2:11.1	910
962	16.23	53.50	—	2:07.6	15.25	49.64	24.2	—	909
961	16.21	53.42	—	—	15.23	49.58	—	2:11.2	908
960	16.19	53.34	—	2:07.7	15.22	49.50	—	2:11.3	907
959	16.17	53.28	—	2:07.8	15.20	49.44	—	—	906
958	16.16	53.20	—	—	15.18	49.36	—	2:11.4	905
957	16.14	53.12	23.8	2:07.9	15.16	49.28	—	2:11.5	904
956	16.12	53.06	—	—	15.14	49.22	—	2:11.6	903
955	16.10	52.98	—	2:08.0	15.13	49.14	—	—	902
954	16.08	52.90	—	2:08.1	15.11	49.08	—	2:11.7	901
953	16.06	52.84	—	—	15.09	49.00	24.3	2:11.8	900
952	16.04	52.76	—	2:08.2	15.07	48.94	—	—	899
951	16.02	52.68	—	2:08.3	15.05	48.86	—	2:11.9	898
950	16.01	52.62	—	—	15.04	48.80	—	2:12.0	897
949	15.99	52.54	—	2:08.4	15.02	48.72	—	2:12.1	896
948	15.97	52.46	—	2:08.5	15.00	48.66	—	—	895
947	15.95	52.40	23.9	—	14.98	48.58	—	2:12.2	894
946	15.93	52.32	—	2:08.6	14.96	48.50	—	2:12.3	893
945	15.91	52.24	—	2:08.7	14.95	48.44	—	—	892
944	15.89	52.18	—	—	14.93	48.36	24.4	2:12.4	891
943	15.88	52.10	—	2:08.8	14.91	48.30	—	2:12.5	890
942	15.86	52.02	—	2:08.9	14.89	48.22	—	—	889
941	15.84	51.96	—	2:09.0	14.87	48.16	—	2:12.6	888
940	15.82	51.88	—	—	14.86	48.08	—	2:12.7	887
939	15.80	51.80	—	2:09.1	14.84	48.02	—	2:12.8	886
938	15.78	51.74	24.0	2:09.2	14.82	47.94	—	—	885
937	15.77	51.66	—	—	14.80	47.88	—	2:12.9	884
936	15.75	51.58	—	2:09.3	14.78	47.80	—	2:13.0	883
935	15.73	51.52	—	2:09.4	14.77	47.74	24.5	—	882
Points	Shot Put	Javelin	200 M	800 M	Shot Put	Javelin	200 M	800 M	Points

SHOT PUT, JAVELIN, 200 M, AND 800 M COMBINED TABLES

Points	Shot Put M	Javelin M	200 M Secs.	800 M Mins.	Shot Put M	Javelin M	200 M Secs.	800 M Mins	Points
881	14.75	47.66	—	2:13.1	13.83	44.10	25.2	2:17.0	829
880	14.73	47.60	—	2:13.2	13.82	44.04	—	—	828
879	14.71	47.52	—	2:13.3	13.80	43.96	—	2:17.1	827
878	14.69	47.46	—	—	13.78	43.90	—	2:17.2	826
877	14.68	47.38	—	2:13.4	13.76	43.84	—	2:17.3	825
876	14.66	47.32	—	2:13.5	13.75	43.76	—	—	824
875	14.64	47.24	—	—	13.73	43.70	—	2:17.4	823
874	14.62	47.18	—	2:13.6	13.71	43.64	—	2:17.5	822
873	14.61	47.10	24.7	2:13.7	13.70	43.56	—	2:17.6	821
872	14.59	47.04	—	2:13.8	13.68	43.50	25.3	—	820
871	14.57	46.98	—	—	13.66	43.44	—	2:17.7	819
870	14.55	46.90	—	2:13.9	13.64	43.36	—	2:17.8	818
869	14.53	46.84	—	2:14.0	13.63	43.30	—	2:17.9	817
868	14.52	46.76	—	2:14.1	13.61	43.24	—	—	816
867	14.50	46.70	—	—	13.59	43.16	—	2:18.0	815
866	14.48	46.62	—	2:14.2	13.58	43.10	—	2:18.1	814
865	14.46	46.56	—	2:14.3	13.56	43.04	—	2:18.2	813
864	14.45	46.48	24.8	—	13.54	42.96	25.4	2:18.3	812
863	14.43	46.42	—	2:14.4	13.52	42.90	—	—	811
862	14.41	46.34	—	2:14.5	13.51	42.84	—	2:18.4	810
861	14.39	46.28	—	2:14.6	13.49	42.76	—	2:18.5	809
860	14.38	46.22	—	—	13.47	42.70	—	2:18.6	808
859	14.36	46.14	—	2:14.7	13.46	42.64	—	—	807
858	14.34	46.08	—	2:14.8	13.44	42.58	—	2:18.7	806
857	14.32	46.00	—	2:14.9	13.42	42.50	—	2:18.8	805
856	14.30	45.94	—	—	13.40	42.44	—	2:18.9	804
855	14.29	45.86	24.9	2:15.0	13.39	42.38	25.5	2:19.0	803
854	14.27	45.80	—	2:15.1	13.37	42.30	—	—	802
853	14.25	45.74	—	2:15.2	13.35	42.24	—	2:19.1	801
852	14.23	45.66	—	—	13.34	42.18	—	2:19.2	800
851	14.22	45.60	—	2:15.3	13.32	42.10	—	2:19.3	799
850	14.20	45.52	—	2:15.4	13.30	42.04	—	—	798
849	14.18	45.46	—	2:15.5	13.29	41.98	—	2:19.4	797
848	14.16	45.38	—	—	13.27	41.92	—	2:19.5	796
847	14.15	45.32	—	2:15.6	13.25	41.84	25.6	2:19.6	795
846	14.13	45.26	25.0	2:15.7	13.24	41.78	—	2:19.7	794
845	14.11	45.18	—	—	13.22	41.72	—	—	793
844	14.09	45.12	—	2:15.8	13.20	41.66	—	2:19.8	792
843	14.08	45.04	—	2:15.9	13.18	41.58	—	2:19.9	791
842	14.06	44.98	—	2:16.0	13.17	41.52	—	2:20.0	790
841	14.04	44.92	—	—	13.15	41.46	—	2:20.1	789
840	14.02	44.84	—	2:16.1	13.13	41.40	—	—	788
839	14.01	44.78	—	2:16.2	13.12	41.32	25.7	2:20.2	787
838	13.99	44.72	25.1	2:16.3	13.10	41.26	—	2:20.3	786
837	13.97	44.64	—	—	13.08	41.20	—	2:20.4	785
836	13.96	44.58	—	2:16.4	13.07	41.14	—	2:20.5	784
835	13.94	44.50	—	2:16.5	13.05	41.06	—	—	783
834	13.92	44.44	—	2:16.6	13.03	41.00	—	2:20.6	782
833	13.90	44.38	—	—	13.02	40.94	—	2:20.7	781
832	13.89	44.30	—	2:16.7	13.00	40.88	—	2:20.8	780
831	13.87	44.24	—	2:16.8	12.98	40.80	25.8	2:20.9	779
					12.97	40.74	—	—	778
830	13.85	44.18	—	2:16.9	12.95	40.68	—	2:21.0	777

SHOT PUT, JAVELIN, 200 M, AND 800 M COMBINED TABLES

Points	Shot Put M	Javelin M	200 M Secs.	800 M Mins.	Shot Put M	Javelin M	200 M Secs.	800 M Mins.	Points
776	12.93	40.62	—	2:21.1	12.06	37.26	26.5	2:25.5	723
775	12.92	40.54	—	2:21.2	12.04	37.20	—	2:25.6	722
774	12.90	40.48	—	2:21.3	12.03	37.14	—	2:25.7	721
773	12.88	40.42	—	—					
772	12.87	40.36	—	2:21.4	12.01	37.08	—	2:25.8	720
771	12.85	40.30	—	2:21.5	12.00	37.02	—	—	719
					11.98	36.96	—	2:25.9	718
770	12.83	40.22	25.9	2:21.6	11.96	36.90	—	2:26.0	717
769	12.82	40.16	—	2:21.7	11.95	36.84	—	2:26.1	716
768	12.80	40.10	—	—	11.93	36.78	26.6	2:26.2	715
767	12.78	40.04	—	2:21.8	11.92	36.72	—	2:26.3	714
766	12.77	39.98	—	2:21.9	11.90	36.66	—	2:26.4	713
765	12.75	39.90	—	2:22.0	11.88	36.58	—	—	712
764	12.73	39.84	—	2:22.1	11.87	36.52	—	2:26.5	711
763	12.72	39.78	—	2:22.2					
762	12.70	39.72	26.0	—	11.85	36.46	—	2:26.6	710
761	12.68	39.66	—	2:22.3	11.84	36.40	—	2:26.7	709
					11.82	36.34	—	2:26.8	708
760	12.67	39.58	—	2:22.4	11.80	36.28	26.7	2:26.9	707
759	12.65	39.52	—	2:22.5	11.79	36.22	—	2:27.0	706
758	12.63	39.46	—	2:22.6	11.77	36.16	—	2:27.1	705
757	12.62	39.40	—	—	11.76	36.10	—	—	704
756	12.60	39.34	—	2:22.7	11.74	36.04	—	2:27.2	703
755	12.58	39.26	—	2:22.8	11.72	35.98	—	2:27.3	702
754	12.57	39.20	26.1	2:22.9	11.71	35.92	—	2:27.4	701
753	12.55	39.14	—	2:23.0					
752	12.53	39.08	—	2:23.1	11.69	35.86	—	2:27.5	700
751	12.52	39.02	—	—	11.68	35.80	26.8	2:27.6	699
					11.66	35.74	—	2:27.7	698
750	12.50	38.96	—	2:23.2	11.64	35.68	—	2:27.8	697
749	12.48	38.90	—	2:23.3	11.63	35.62	—	—	696
748	12.47	38.82	—	2:23.4	11.61	35.56	—	2:27.9	695
747	12.45	38.76	—	2:23.5	11.60	35.50	—	2:28.0	694
746	12.44	38.70	26.2	2:23.6	11.58	35.44	—	2:28.1	693
745	12.42	38.64	—	—	11.57	35.38	26.9	2:28.2	692
744	12.40	38.58	—	2:23.7	11.55	35.32	—	2:28.3	691
743	12.39	38.52	—	2:23.8					
742	12.37	38.44	—	2:23.9	11.53	35.26	—	2:28.4	690
741	12.35	38.38	—	2:24.0	11.52	35.20	—	2:28.5	689
					11.50	35.14	—	2:28.6	688
740	12.34	38.32	—	2:24.1	11.49	35.08	—	—	687
739	12.32	38.26	—	—	11.47	35.02	—	2:28.7	686
738	12.30	38.20	26.3	2:24.2	11.46	34.96	—	2:28.8	685
737	12.29	38.14	—	2:24.3	11.44	34.90	27.0	2:28.9	684
736	12.27	38.08	—	2:24.4	11.42	34.84	—	2:29.0	683
735	12.26	38.02	—	2:24.5	11.41	34.78	—	2:29.1	682
734	12.24	37.94	—	2:24.6	11.39	34.72	—	2:29.2	681
733	12.22	37.88	—	—					
732	12.21	37.82	—	2:24.7	11.38	34.66	—	2:29.3	680
731	12.19	37.76	—	2:24.8	11.36	34.60	—	2:29.4	679
					11.35	34.54	—	2:29.5	678
730	12.17	37.70	26.4	2:24.9	11.33	34.48	27.1	—	677
729	12.16	37.64	—	2:25.0	11.31	34.42	—	2:29.6	676
728	12.14	37.58	—	2:25.1	11.30	34.36	—	2:29.7	675
727	12.13	37.52	—	2:25.2	11.28	34.30	—	2:29.8	674
726	12.11	37.46	—	—	11.27	34.24	—	2:29.9	673
725	12.09	37.40	—	2:25.3	11.25	34.18	—	2:30.0	672
724	12.08	37.32	—	2:25.4	11.24	34.12	—	2:30.1	671
Points	Shot Put	Javelin	200 M	800 M	Shot Put	Javelin	200 M	800 M	Points

SHOT PUT, JAVELIN, 200 M, AND 800 M COMBINED TABLES

Points	Shot Put M	Javelin M	200 M Secs.	800 M Mins.	Shot Put M	Javelin M	200 M Secs.	800 M Mins.	Points
670	11.22	34.06	—	2:30.2	10.41	31.00	—	2:35.2	617
669	11.20	34.00	27.2	2:30.3	10.39	30.94	—	2:35.3	616
668	11.19	33.94	—	2:30.4	10.38	30.90	—	2:35.4	615
667	11.17	33.88	—	2:30.5	10.36	30.84	—	2:35.5	614
666	11.16	33.82	—	—	10.35	30.78	—	2:35.6	613
665	11.14	33.76	—	2:30.6	10.33	30.72	28.0	2:35.7	612
664	11.13	33.72	—	2:30.7	10.32	30.66	—	2:35.8	611
663	11.11	33.66	—	2:30.8	10.30	30.62	—	2:35.9	610
662	11.10	33.60	27.3	2:30.9	10.29	30.56	—	2:36.0	609
661	11.08	33.54	—	2:31.0	10.28	30.50	—	2:36.1	608
660	11.06	33.48	—	2:31.1	10.26	30.44	—	2:36.2	607
659	11.05	33.42	—	2:31.2	10.25	30.38	—	2:36.3	606
658	11.03	33.36	—	2:31.3	10.23	30.34	28.1	2:36.4	605
657	11.02	33.30	—	2:31.4	10.22	30.28	—	2:36.5	604
656	11.00	33.24	—	2:31.5	10.20	30.22	—	2:36.6	603
655	10.99	33.18	27.4	2:31.6	10.19	30.16	—	2:36.7	602
654	10.97	33.12	—	2:31.7	10.17	30.12	—	2:36.8	601
653	10.96	33.06	—	2:31.8	10.16	30.06	—	2:36.9	600
652	10.94	33.00	—	—	10.14	30.00	—	2:37.0	599
651	10.93	32.96	—	2:31.9	10.13	29.94	28.2	2:37.1	598
650	10.91	32.90	—	2:32.0	10.11	29.88	—	2:37.2	597
649	10.90	32.84	—	2:32.1	10.10	29.84	—	2:37.3	596
648	10.88	32.78	—	2:32.2	10.08	29.78	—	2:37.4	595
647	10.86	32.72	27.5	2:32.3	10.07	29.72	—	2:37.5	594
646	10.85	32.66	—	2:32.4	10.05	29.66	—	2:37.6	593
645	10.83	32.60	—	2:32.5	10.04	29.62	—	2:37.7	592
644	10.82	32.54	—	2:32.6	10.02	29.56	28.3	2:37.8	591
643	10.80	32.48	—	2:32.7	10.01	29.50	—	2:37.9	590
642	10.79	32.44	—	2:32.8	9.99	29.44	—	2:38.0	589
641	10.77	32.38	—	2:32.9	9.98	29.40	—	2:38.1	588
640	10.76	32.32	27.6	2:33.0	9.96	29.34	—	2:38.2	587
639	10.74	32.26	—	2:33.1	9.95	29.28	—	2:38.3	586
638	10.73	32.20	—	2:33.2	9.94	29.22	—	2:38.4	585
637	10.71	32.14	—	2:33.3	9.92	29.18	28.4	2:38.5	584
636	10.70	32.08	—	2:33.4	9.91	29.12	—	2:38.6	583
635	10.68	32.02	—	—	9.89	29.06	—	2:38.7	582
634	10.67	31.98	—	2:33.5	9.88	29.00	—	2:38.8	581
633	10.65	31.92	27.7	2:33.6	9.86	28.96	—	2:38.9	580
632	10.64	31.86	—	2:33.7	9.85	28.90	—	2:39.0	579
631	10.62	31.80	—	2:33.8	9.83	28.84	28.5	2:39.1	578
630	10.61	31.74	—	2:33.9	9.82	28.80	—	2:39.2	577
629	10.59	31.68	—	2:34.0	9.80	28.74	—	2:39.3	576
628	10.58	31.62	—	2:34.1	9.79	28.68	—	2:39.4	575
627	10.56	31.58	—	2:34.2	9.77	28.62	—	2:39.5	574
626	10.55	31.52	27.8	2:34.3	9.76	28.58	—	2:39.6	573
625	10.53	31.46	—	2:34.4	9.75	28.52	—	2:39.7	572
624	10.52	31.40	—	2:34.5	9.73	28.46	28.6	2:39.8	571
623	10.50	31.34	—	2:34.6	9.72	28.42	—	2:39.9	570
622	10.48	31.28	—	2:34.7	9.70	28.36	—	2:40.0	569
621	10.47	31.24	—	2:34.8	9.69	28.30	—	2:40.1	568
620	10.45	31.18	—	2:34.9	9.67	28.26	—	2:40.2	567
619	10.44	31.12	27.9	2:35.0	9.66	28.20	—	2:40.3	566
618	10.42	31.06	—	2:35.1	9.64	28.14	—	2:40.4	565

SHOT PUT, JAVELIN, 200 M, AND 800 M COMBINED TABLES

Points	Shot Put M	Javelin M	200 M Secs.	800 M Mins.	Shot Put M	Javelin M	200 M Secs.	800 M Mins.	Points
564	9.63	28.10	28.7	2:40.5	8.87	25.26	—	2:46.4	510
563	9.62	28.04	—	2:40.6	8.85	25.22	—	2:46.5	509
562	9.60	27.98	—	2:40.7	8.84	25.16	—	2:46.6	508
561	9.59	27.92	—	2:40.8	8.82	25.12	—	2:46.7	507
560	9.57	27.88	—	2:40.9	8.81	25.06	29.6	2:46.8	506
559	9.56	27.82	—	2:41.0	8.80	25.02	—	2:46.9	505
558	9.54	27.76	28.8	2:41.2	8.78	24.96	—	2:47.0	504
557	9.53	27.72	—	2:41.3	8.77	24.92	—	2:47.1	503
556	9.51	27.66	—	2:41.4	8.76	24.86	—	2:47.3	502
555	9.50	27.60	—	2:41.5	8.74	24.82	—	2:47.4	501
554	9.49	27.56	—	2:41.6	8.73	24.76	29.7	2:47.5	500
553	9.47	27.50	—	2:41.7	8.71	24.72	—	2:47.6	499
552	9.46	27.46	—	2:41.8	8.70	24.66	—	2:47.7	498
551	9.44	27.40	28.9	2:41.9	8.69	24.62	29.8	2:47.8	497
550	9.43	27.34	—	2:42.0	8.67	24.56	—	2:47.9	496
549	9.41	27.30	—	2:42.1	8.66	24.52	—	2:48.1	495
548	9.40	27.24	—	2:42.2	8.65	24.46	—	2:48.2	494
547	9.39	27.18	—	2:42.3	8.63	24.42	—	2:48.3	493
546	9.37	27.14	—	2:42.4	8.62	24.36	—	2:48.4	492
545	9.36	27.08	29.0	2:42.5	8.60	24.32	29.9	2:48.5	491
544	9.34	27.02	—	2:42.6	8.59	24.26	—	2:48.6	490
543	9.33	26.98	—	2:42.7	8.58	24.22	—	2:48.7	489
542	9.31	26.92	—	2:42.8	8.56	24.16	—	2:48.9	488
541	9.30	26.88	—	2:43.0	8.55	24.12	—	2:49.0	487
540	9.29	26.82	—	2:43.1	8.54	24.06	—	2:49.1	486
539	9.27	26.76	—	2:43.2	8.52	24.02	—	2:49.2	485
538	9.26	26.72	29.1	2:43.3	8.51	23.96	30.0	2:49.3	484
537	9.24	26.66	—	2:43.4	8.50	23.92	—	2:49.4	483
536	9.23	26.60	—	2:43.5	8.48	23.86	—	2:49.6	482
535	9.22	26.56	—	2:43.6	8.47	23.82	—	2:49.7	481
534	9.20	26.50	—	2:43.7	8.46	23.76	—	2:49.8	480
533	9.19	26.46	—	2:43.8	8.44	23.72	—	2:49.9	479
532	9.17	26.40	29.2	2:43.9	8.43	23.66	30.1	2:50.0	478
531	9.16	26.34	—	2:44.0	8.41	23.62	—	2:50.1	477
530	9.15	26.30	—	2:44.1	8.40	23.56	—	2:50.3	476
529	9.13	26.24	—	2:44.3	8.39	23.52	—	2:50.4	475
528	9.12	26.20	—	2:44.4	8.37	23.48	—	2:50.5	474
527	9.10	26.14	—	2:44.5	8.36	23.42	—	2:50.6	473
526	9.09	26.08	—	2:44.6	8.34	23.38	3.02	2:50.7	472
525	9.08	26.04	29.3	2:44.7	8.33	23.32	—	2:50.8	471
524	9.06	25.98	—	2:44.8	8.32	23.28	—	2:51.0	470
523	9.05	25.94	—	2:44.9	8.31	23.22	—	2:51.1	469
522	9.03	25.88	—	2:45.0	8.29	23.18	—	2:51.2	468
521	9.02	25.84	—	2:45.1	8.28	23.12	—	2:51.3	467
520	9.01	25.78	—	2:45.2	8.27	23.08	30.3	2:51.4	466
519	8.99	25.72	29.4	2:45.4	8.25	23.04	—	2:51.6	465
518	8.98	25.68	—	2:45.5	8.24	22.98	—	2:51.7	464
517	8.96	25.62	—	2:45.6	8.23	22.94	—	2:51.8	463
516	8.95	25.58	—	2:45.7	8.21	22.88	—	2:51.9	462
515	8.94	25.52	—	2:45.8	8.20	22.84	—	2:52.0	461
514	8.92	25.48	—	2:45.9	8.19	22.78	30.4	2:52.1	460
513	8.91	25.42	29.5	2:46.0	8.17	22.74	—	2:52.3	459
512	8.89	25.38	—	2:46.1	8.16	22.70	—	2:52.4	458
511	8.88	25.32	—	2:46.2					

SHOT PUT, JAVELIN, 200 M, AND 800 M COMBINED TABLES

Points	Shot Put M	Javelin M	200 M Secs.	800 M Mins.	Shot Put M	Javelin M	200 M Secs.	800 M Mins.	Points
457	8.15	22.64	—	2:52.5	7.46	20.16	—	2:59.1	404
456	8.13	22.60	—	2:52.6	7.45	20.12	31.4	2:59.3	403
455	8.12	22.54	—	2:52.8	7.43	20.08	—	2:59.4	402
454	8.11	22.50	30.5	2:52.9	7.42	20.02	—	2:59.5	401
453	8.09	22.46	—	2:53.0	7.41	19.98	—	2:59.7	400
452	8.08	22.40	—	2:53.1	7.40	19.94	—	2:59.8	399
451	8.07	22.36	—	2:53.2	7.38	19.90	—	2:59.9	398
450	8.05	22.30	—	2:53.4	7.37	19.84	31.5	3:00.0	397
449	8.04	22.26	30.6	2:53.5	7.36	19.80	—	3:00.2	396
448	8.03	22.22	—	2:53.6	7.35	19.76	—	3:00.3	395
447	8.02	22.16	—	2:53.7	7.33	19.72	—	3:00.4	394
446	8.00	22.12	—	2:53.8	7.32	19.66	—	3:00.6	393
445	7.99	22.08	—	2:54.0	7.31	19.62	31.6	3:00.7	392
444	7.98	22.02	—	2:54.1	7.29	19.58	—	3:00.8	391
443	7.96	21.98	30.7	2:54.2	7.28	19.54	—	3:01.0	390
442	7.95	21.92	—	2:54.3	7.27	19.48	—	3:01.1	389
441	7.94	21.88	—	2:54.5	7.26	19.44	—	3:01.2	388
440	7.92	21.84	—	2:54.6	7.24	19.40	—	3:01.4	387
439	7.91	21.78	—	2:54.7	7.23	19.36	31.7	3:01.5	386
438	7.90	21.74	—	2:54.8	7.22	19.30	—	3:01.6	385
437	7.88	21.70	30.8	2:55.0	7.21	19.26	—	3:01.8	384
436	7.87	21.64	—	2:55.1	7.19	19.22	—	3:01.9	383
435	7.86	21.60	—	2:55.2	7.18	19.18	—	3:02.0	382
434	7.84	21.56	—	2:55.3	7.17	19.14	31.8	3:02.2	381
433	7.83	21.50	—	2:55.4	7.16	19.08	—	3:02.3	380
432	7.82	21.46	—	2:55.6	7.14	19.04	—	3:02.4	379
431	7.81	21.40	30.9	2:55.7	7.13	19.00	—	3:02.6	378
430	7.79	21.36	—	2:55.8	7.12	18.96	—	3:02.7	377
429	7.78	21.32	—	2:55.9	7.11	18.92	—	3:02.8	376
428	7.77	21.26	—	2:56.1	7.10	18.86	31.9	3:03.0	375
427	7.75	21.22	—	2:56.2	7.08	18.82	—	3:03.1	374
426	7.74	21.18	—	2:56.3	7.07	18.78	—	3:03.3	373
425	7.73	21.12	31.0	2:56.5	7.06	18.74	—	3:03.4	372
424	7.72	21.08	—	2:56.6	7.05	18.70	—	3:03.5	371
423	7.70	21.04	—	2:56.7	7.03	18.64	32.0	3:03.7	370
422	7.69	21.00	—	2:56.8	7.02	18.60	—	3:03.8	369
421	7.68	20.94	—	2:57.0	7.01	18.56	—	3:03.9	368
420	7.66	20.90	31.1	2:57.1	7.00	18.52	—	3:04.1	367
419	7.65	20.86	—	2:57.2	6.98	18.48	—	3:04.2	366
418	7.64	20.80	—	2:57.3	6.97	18.44	32.1	3:04.3	365
417	7.62	20.76	—	2:57.5	6.96	18.38	—	3:04.5	364
416	7.61	20.72	—	2:57.6	6.95	18.34	—	3:04.6	363
415	7.60	20.66	—	2:57.7	6.93	18.30	—	3:04.8	362
414	7.59	20.62	31.2	2:57.8	6.92	18.26	—	3:04.9	361
413	7.57	20.58	—	2:58.0	6.91	18.22	—	3:05.0	360
412	7.56	20.52	—	2:58.1	6.90	18.18	32.2	3:05.2	359
411	7.55	20.48	—	2:58.2	6.89	18.12	—	3:05.3	358
410	7.54	20.44	—	2:58.4	6.87	18.08	—	3:05.5	357
409	7.52	20.40	—	2:58.5	6.86	18.04	—	3:05.6	356
408	7.51	20.34	31.3	2:58.6	6.85	18.00	—	3:05.7	355
407	7.50	20.30	—	2:58.7	6.84	17.96	32.3	3:05.9	354
406	7.48	20.26	—	2:58.9	6.83	17.92	—	3:06.0	353
405	7.47	20.20	—	2:59.0	6.81	17.88	—	3:06.2	352
Points	Shot Put	Javelin	200 M	800 M	Shot Put	Javelin	200 M	800 M	Points

Points	Shot Put M	Javelin M	200 M Secs.	800 M Mins.	Shot Put M	Javelin M	200 M Secs.	800 M Mins	Points
351	6.80	17.82	—	3:06.3	6.18	15.68	—	3:13.9	299
					6.17	15.64	33.4	3:14.0	298
350	6.79	17.78	—	3:06.4	6.16	15.60	—	3:14.2	297
349	6.78	17.74	32.4	3:06.6	6.15	15.56	—	3:14.3	296
348	6.76	17.70	—	3:06.7	6.14	15.52	—	3:14.5	295
347	6.75	17.66	—	3:06.9	6.13	15.48	—	3:14.7	294
346	6.74	17.62	—	3:07.0	6.12	15.44	33.5	3:14.8	293
345	6.73	17.58	—	3:07.1	6.10	15.40	—	3:15.0	292
344	6.72	17.52	32.5	3:07.3	6.09	15.36	—	3:15.1	291
343	6.70	17.48	—	3:07.4	6.08	15.32	—	3:15.3	290
342	6.69	17.44	—	3:07.6	6.07	15.28	—	3:15.4	289
341	6.68	17.40	—	3:07.7	6.06	15.24	33.6	3:15.6	288
340	6.67	17.36	—	3:07.8	6.05	15.20	—	3:15.7	287
339	6.66	17.32	32.6	3:08.0	6.04	15.16	—	3:15.9	286
338	6.64	17.28	—	3:08.1	6.02	15.12	—	3:16.0	285
337	6.63	17.24	—	3:08.3	6.01	15.08	33.7	3:16.2	284
336	6.62	17.20	—	3:08.4	6.00	15.04	—	3:16.4	283
335	6.61	17.16	—	3:08.6	5.99	15.00	—	3:16.5	282
334	6.60	17.10	—	3:08.7	5.98	14.96	—	3.16.7	281
333	6.58	17.06	32.7	3:08.9	5.97	14.92	—	3:16.8	280
332	6.57	17.02	—	3:09.0	5.96	14.88	33.8	3:17.0	279
331	6.56	16.98	—	3:09.1	5.94	14.84	—	3:17.1	278
330	6.55	16.94	—	3:09.3	5.93	14.80	—	3:17.3	277
329	6.54	16.90	—	3:09.4	5.92	14.76	—	3:17.5	276
328	6.52	16.86	32.8	3:09.6	5.91	14.72	—	3:17.6	275
327	6.51	16.82	—	3:09.7	5.90	14.68	33.9	3:17.8	274
326	6.50	16.78	—	3:09.9	5.89	14.66	—	3:17.9	273
325	6.49	16.74	—	3:10.0	5.88	14.62	—	3:18.1	272
324	6.48	16.70	—	3:10.2	5.87	14.58	—	3:18.2	271
323	6.47	16.66	32.9	3:10.3	5.85	14.54	—	3:18.4	270
322	6.45	16.60	—	3:10.5	5.84	14.50	34.0	3:18.6	269
321	6.44	16.56	—	3:10.6	5.83	14.46	—	3:18.7	268
320	6.43	16.52	—	3:10.7	5.82	14.42	—	3:18.9	267
319	6.42	16.48	—	3:10.9	5.81	14.38	—	3:19.0	266
318	6.41	16.44	33.0	3:11.0	5.80	14.34	34.1	3:19.2	265
317	6.39	16.40	—	3:11.2	5.79	14.30	—	3:19.4	264
316	6.38	16.36	—	3:11.3	5.78	14.26	—	3:19.5	263
315	6.37	16.32	—	3:11.5	5.76	14.22	—	3:19.7	262
314	6.36	16.28	—	3:11.6	5.75	14.18	—	3:19.8	261
313	6.35	16.24	33.1	3:11.8	5.74	14.16	34.2	3:20.0	260
312	6.34	16.20	—	3:11.9	5.73	14.12	—	3:20.2	259
311	6.32	16.16	—	3:12.1	5.72	14.08	—	3:20.3	258
310	6.31	16.12	—	3:12.2	5.71	14.04	—	3:20.5	257
309	6.30	16.08	—	3:12.4	5.70	14.00	—	3:20.7	256
308	6.29	16.04	33.2	3:12.5	5.69	13.96	34.3	3:20.8	255
307	6.28	16.00	—	3:12.7	5.68	13.92	—	3:21.0	254
306	6.27	15.96	—	3:12.8	5.66	13.88	—	3:21.1	253
305	6.25	15.92	—	3:13.0	5.65	13.84	—	3:21.3	252
304	6.24	15.88	—	3:13.1	5.64	13.82	34.4	3:21.5	251
303	6.23	15.84	33.3	3:13.3	5.63	13.78	—	3:21.6	250
302	6.22	15.80	—	3:13.4	5.62	13.74	—	3:21.8	249
301	6.21	15.76	—	3:13.6	5.61	13.70	—	3:22.0	248
300	6.20	15.72	—	3:13.7	5.60	13.66	—	3:22.1	247
Points	Shot Put	Javelin	200 M	800 M	Shot Put	Javelin	200 M	800 M	Points

Points	Shot Put M	Javelin M	200 M Secs.	800 M Mins.	Shot Put M	Javelin M	200 M Secs.	800 M Mins.	Points
246	5.59	13.62	34.5	3:22.3	5.02	11.72	—	3:31.5	193
245	5.58	13.58	—	3:22.5	5.01	11.68	35.7	3:31.7	192
244	5.57	13.54	—	3:22.6	5.00	11.64	—	3:31.8	191
243	5.55	13.52	—	3:22.8	4.99	11.62	—	3:32.0	190
242	5.54	13.48	—	3:23.0	4.98	11.58	—	3:32.2	189
241	5.53	13.44	34.6	3:23.1	4.97	11.54	35.8	3:32.4	188
240	5.52	13.40	—	3:23.3	4.96	11.50	—	3:32.6	187
239	5.51	13.36	—	3:23.5	4.95	11.48	—	3:32.7	186
238	5.50	13.32	—	3:23.6	4.94	11.44	—	3:32.9	185
237	5.49	13.28	34.7	3:23.8	4.93	11.40	35.9	3:33.1	184
236	5.48	13.26	—	3:24.0	4.92	11.38	—	3:33.3	183
235	5.47	13.22	—	3:24.1	4.91	11.34	—	3:33.5	182
234	5.46	13.18	—	3:24.3	4.90	11.30	—	3:33.7	181
233	5.45	13.14	—	3:24.5	4.89	11.26	36.0	3:33.9	180
232	5.43	13.10	34.8	3:24.6	4.87	11.24	—	3:34.0	179
231	5.42	13.06	—	3:24.8	4.86	11.20	—	3:34.2	178
230	5.41	13.04	—	3:25.0	4.85	11.16	—	3:34.4	177
229	5.40	13.00	—	3:25.2	4.84	11.14	—	3:34.6	176
228	5.39	12.96	34.9	3:25.3	4.83	11.10	36.1	3:34.8	175
227	5.38	12.92	—	3:25.5	4.82	11.06	—	3:35.0	174
226	5.37	12.88	—	3:25.7	4.81	11.04	—	3:35.2	173
225	5.36	12.86	—	3:25.8	4.80	11.00	—	3:35.3	172
224	5.35	12.82	—	3:26.0	4.79	10.96	36.2	3:35.5	171
223	5.34	12.78	35.0	3:26.2	4.78	10.94	—	3:35.7	170
222	5.33	12.74	—	3:26.4	4.77	10.90	—	3:35.9	169
221	5.32	12.70	—	3:26.5	4.76	10.86	—	3:36.1	168
220	5.30	12.66	—	3:26.7	4.75	10.84	36.3	3:36.3	167
219	5.29	12.64	35.1	3:26.9	4.74	10.80	—	3:36.5	166
218	5.28	12.60	—	3:27.0	4.73	10.76	—	3:36.7	165
217	5.27	12.56	—	3:27.2	4.72	10.74	—	3:36.9	164
216	5.26	12.52	—	3:27.4	4.71	10.70	36.4	3:37.0	163
215	5.25	12.50	—	3:27.6	4.70	10.66	—	3:37.2	162
214	5.24	12.46	35.2	3:27.7	4.69	10.64	—	3:37.4	161
213	5.23	12.42	—	3:27.9	4.68	10.60	—	3:37.6	160
212	5.22	12.38	—	3:28.1	4.67	10.56	36.5	3:37.8	159
211	5.21	12.34	—	3:28.3	4.66	10.54	—	3:38.0	158
210	5.20	12.32	35.3	3:28.4	4.65	10.50	—	3:38.2	157
209	5.19	12.28	—	3:28.6	4.64	10.46	—	3:38.4	156
208	5.18	12.24	—	3:28.8	4.63	10.44	36.6	3:38.6	155
207	5.17	12.20	—	3:29.0	4.62	10.40	—	3:38.8	154
206	5.16	12.18	—	3:29.1	4.61	10.38	—	3:39.0	153
205	5.15	12.14	35.4	3:29.3	4.60	10.34	—	3:39.2	152
204	5.13	12.10	—	3:29.5	4.59	10.30	36.7	3:39.4	151
203	5.12	12.06	—	3:29.7	4.58	10.28	—	3:39.6	150
202	5.11	12.02	—	3:29.9	4.57	10.24	—	3:39.7	149
201	5.10	12.00	35.5	3:30.0	4.56	10.20	—	3:39.9	148
200	5.09	11.96	—	3:30.2	4.55	10.18	36.8	3:40.1	147
199	5.08	11.92	—	3:30.4	4.54	10.14	—	3:40.3	146
198	5.07	11.88	—	3:30.6	4.53	10.12	—	3:40.5	145
197	5.06	11.86	35.6	3:30.8	4.52	10.08	—	3:40.7	144
196	5.05	11.82	—	3:30.9	4.51	10.04	36.9	3:40.9	143
195	5.04	11.78	—	3:31.1	4.50	10.02	—	3:41.1	142
194	5.03	11.76	—	3:31.3	4.49	9.98	—	3:41.3	141
Points	Shot Put	Javelin	200 M	800 M	Shot Put	Javelin	200 M	800 M	Points

SHOT PUT, JAVELIN, 200 M, AND 800 M COMBINED TABLES

Points	Shot Put M	Javelin M	200 M Secs.	800 M Mins.	Shot Put M	Javelin M	200 M Secs.	800 M Mins.	Points
140	4.48	9.96	—	3:41.5	3.98	8.34	—	3:52.6	87
139	4.47	9.92	—	3:41.7	3.97	8.30	—	3:52.8	86
138	4.46	9.88	37.0	3:41.9	3.96	8.28	—	3:53.0	85
137	4.45	9.86	—	3:42.1	3.95	8.24	38.4	3:53.2	84
136	4.44	9.82	—	3:42.3	3.94	8.22	—	3:53.4	83
135	4.43	9.80	37.1	3:42.5	3.93	8.18	—	3:53.7	82
134	4.42	9.76	—	3:42.7	3.92	8.16	38.5	3:53.9	81
133	4.41	9.72	—	3:42.9	3.91	8.12	—	3:54.1	80
132	4.40	9.70	—	3:43.1	3.90	8.10	—	3:54.3	79
131	4.39	9.66	37.2	3:43.3	3.89	8.08	—	3:54.6	78
130	4.38	9.64	—	3:43.5	3.88	8.04	38.6	3:54.8	77
129	4.37	9.60	—	3:43.7	3.87	8.02	—	3:55.0	76
128	—	9.58	—	3:43.9	—	7.98	—	3:55.2	75
127	4.36	9.54	37.3	3:44.1	3.86	7.96	—	3:55.4	74
126	4.35	9.52	—	3:44.3	3.85	7.92	38.7	3:55.7	73
125	4.34	9.48	—	3:44.5	3.84	7.90	—	3:55.9	72
124	4.33	9.44	—	3:44.7	3.83	7.88	—	3:56.1	71
123	4.32	9.42	37.4	3:44.9	3.82	7.84	38.8	3:56.3	70
122	4.31	9.38	—	3:45.2	3.81	7.82	—	3:56.6	69
121	4.30	9.36	—	3:45.4	3.80	7.78	—	3:56.8	68
120	4.29	9.32	—	3:45.6	3.79	7.76	—	3:57.0	67
119	4.28	9.30	37.5	3:45.8	3.78	7.74	38.9	3:57.3	66
118	4.27	9.26	—	3:46.0	3.77	7.70	—	3:57.5	65
117	4.26	9.24	—	3:46.2	—	7.68	—	3:57.7	64
116	4.25	9.20	—	3:46.4	3.76	7.64	39.0	3:57.9	63
115	4.24	9.16	37.6	3:46.6	3.75	7.62	—	3:58.2	62
114	4.23	9.14	—	3:46.8	3.74	7.60	—	3:58.4	61
113	4.22	9.10	—	3:47.0	3.73	7.56	—	3:58.6	60
112	4.21	9.08	—	3:47.2	3.72	7.54	39.1	3:58.9	59
111	4.20	9.04	37.7	3:47.4	3.71	7.50	—	3:59.1	58
110	4.19	9.02	—	3:47.6	3.70	7.48	—	3:59.3	57
109	4.18	8.98	—	3:47.8	3.69	7.46	—	3:59.6	56
108	4.17	8.96	—	3:48.1	3.68	7.42	39.2	3:59.8	55
107	4.16	8.92	37.8	3:48.3	—	7.40	—	4:00.0	54
106	4.15	8.90	—	3:48.5	3.67	7.36	—	4:00.3	53
105	4.14	8.88	—	3:48.7	3.66	7.34	39.3	4:00.5	52
104	—	8.84	—	3:48.9	3.65	7.32	—	4:00.7	51
103	4.13	8.80	37.9	3:49.1	3.64	7.28	—	4:01.0	50
102	4.12	8.78	—	3:49.3	3.63	7.26	—	4:01.2	49
101	4.11	8.74	—	3:49.5	3.62	7.24	39.4	4:01.4	48
100	4.10	8.72	—	3:49.8	3.61	7.20	—	4:01.7	47
99	4.09	8.68	38.0	3:50.0	3.60	7.18	—	4:01.9	46
98	4.08	8.66	—	3:50.2	—	7.16	39.5	4:02.1	45
97	4.07	8.62	—	3:50.4	3.59	7.12	—	4:02.4	44
96	4.06	8.60	38.1	3:50.6	3.58	7.10	—	4:02.6	43
95	4.05	8.56	—	3:50.8	3.57	7.06	—	4:02.8	42
94	4.04	8.54	—	3:51.0	3.56	7.04	39.6	4:03.1	41
93	4.03	8.50	—	3:51.3	3.55	7.02	—	4:03.3	40
92	4.02	8.48	38.2	3:51.5	3.54	6.98	—	4:03.6	39
91	4.01	8.44	—	3:51.7	3.53	6.96	39.7	4:03.8	38
90	4.00	8.42	—	3:51.9	3.52	6.94	—	4:04.0	37
89	3.99	8.40	—	3:52.1	—	6.90	—	4:04.3	36
88	—	8.36	38.3	3:52.3	3.51	6.88	—	4:04.5	35
Points	Shot Put	Javelin	200 M	800 M	Shot Put	Javelin	200 M	800 M	Points

SHOT PUT, JAVELIN, 200 M, AND 800 M COMBINED TABLES

Points	Shot Put M	Javelin M	200 M Secs.	800 M Mins.	Shot Put M	Javelin M	200 M Secs.	800 M Mins.	Points
34	3.50	6.86	39.8	4:04.8	3.35	6.42	40.3	4:09.0	17
33	3.49	6.82	—	4:05.0	3.34	6.38	—	4:09.2	16
32	3.48	6.80	—	4:05.3	—	6.36	—	4:09.5	15
31	3.47	6.78	39.9	4:05.5	3.33	6.34	40.4	4:09.7	14
30	3.46	6.76	—	4:05.7	3.32	6.32	—	4:10.0	13
29	—	6.72	—	4:06.0	3.31	6.28	—	4:10.2	12
28	3.45	6.70	—	4:06.2	3.30	6.25	—	4:10.5	11
27	3.44	6.68	40.0	4:06.5	3.29	6.24	40.5	4:10.7	10
26	3.43	6.64	—	4:06.7	—	6.20	—	4:11.0	9
25	3.42	6.62	—	4:07.0	3.28	6.18	—	4:11.2	8
24	3.41	6.60	40.1	4:07.2	3.27	6.16	40.6	4:11.5	7
23	3.40	6.56	—	4:07.5	3.26	6.14	—	4:11.8	6
22	—	6.54	—	4:07.7	3.25	6.10	—	4:12.0	5
21	3.39	6.52	40.2	4:08.0	3.24	6.08	40.7	4:12.3	4
20	3.38	6.50	—	4:08.2	—	6.06	—	4:12.5	3
19	3.37	6.46	—	4:08.5	3.23	6.04	—	4:12.8	2
18	3.36	6.44	—	4:08.7	3.22	6.00	—	4:13.0	1
Points	Shot Put	Javelin	200 M	800 M	Shot Put	Javelin	200 M	800 M	Points

Officiating

NAGWS Affiliated
Boards of Officials

The Affiliated Boards of Officials (ABO) is one of 6 structures of the National Association for Girls and Women in Sport (NAGWS). The following official statement of goals was approved by the ABO Executive Council (Fall, 1977) in an effort to clarify the future directions of ABO:

1. To improve the quality of officiating for girls' and women's sports contests, regardless of the level of skill/maturity of players, or the rules governing the contest.
2. To increase the number of competent women officials, not to the exclusion of men, but as needed affirmative action.
3. To promote the involvement of women in the governing bodies of other sports officiating groups.

The purpose of the ABO is to promote quality officiating for girls' and women's sport programs by:

(1) Developing officiating techniques
(2) Providing materials for training and rating officials
(3) Disseminating information about officiating
(4) Promoting the use of ABO-rated officials
(5) Developing standards of conduct for officials compatible with the philosophy of the NAGWS
(6) Providing the organizational and administrative structure for the coordination of Affiliated Boards
(7) Promoting standards with respect to fees, ratings, and uniforms.

Approximately 250 Boards of Officials throughout the United States are affiliated with NAGWS/ABO. These boards provide opportunities for interested individuals to learn about officiating or judging and are authorized to give NAGWS ratings.

The Principles and Techniques of Officiating (PTO) Committees for each of the 9 sports in which ABO grants ratings are specifically concerned with enumerating the mechanics used by referees, umpires, and judges in officiating games, meets, or matches.

The Examinations and Ratings (E & R) Committees for each of the 9 sports in which ABO grants ratings are responsible for preparing, revising, and analyzing the officiating theoretical (written) examinations.

ABO EXECUTIVE COUNCIL

ABO Executive Committee
  Sandy Abbinanti *Past Chair*
  Marcia Saneholtz *Chair*
  Carol L. Thompson *NAGWS Executive Director* (ex-officio)
ABO Sport Representatives
  Julie Doherty *High School Representative*
  June L. Courteau *Basketball Representative*
  Cheryl Hamilton *Gymnastics Representative*
  Sandy Cutter *Soccer Representative*
  Loretta Dressler *Softball Representative*
  Chris Jackson *Swimming/Diving Representative*
  (to be appointed) *Sync. Swimming Representative*
  (to be appointed) *Track & Field Representative*
  Debbie Chin *Volleyball Representative*

If you have questions concerning the techniques of officiating *track and field* write to:

> LURLINE JONES
> 940 E. McPherson St.
> Philadelphia, PA 19150

Information regarding *track and field* study questions in this Track and Field Guide or on the track and field theoretical examinations should be addressed to:

> CLAUDIA BLACKMAN
> Southern Illinois University
> Dept. of Physical Education
> Carbondale, IL 62901

Additional information regarding ABO officiating concerns may be secured by writing:

> Affiliated Boards of Officials
> ABO Program Administrator
> 1900 Association Dr.
> Reston, VA 22091
> (703) 476-3451

The *ABO Directory/Handbook* may be purchased for $3.00 from:

> NAGWS
> 1900 Association Dr.
> Reston, VA 22091
> (703) 476-3450

Statement of Philosophy of the Affiliated Boards of Officials

The Role of the Official in the Competitive Situation

Educational values should be of primary concern to all who have leadership roles in a competitive program. As one of those fulfilling leadership roles, the official must be concerned with promoting those values and with the welfare of the participant. The unique contribution of the official is assuring equal opportunity and fair play for all. The official essentially acts as an arbitrator, providing judgments that are within the spirit and intent of the rules. Decisions are based on objective evidence, free from bias and from the emotion that often pervades the competitive environment.

An official enters the competitive situation with a thorough understanding of the letter, as well as the intent of the rules, the strategy and skills of the sport to be played, and correct execution of officiating techniques to view the contest accurately. The official maintains a friendly yet reserved attitude toward all throughout the sport experience. The official is flexible, operating within officiating standards appropriate to the age of the performers, the level of skill, and the facilities available. Biases by players, spectators, and coaches will be evaluated with an understanding not only of the multiplicity of ways in which individuals may react to a competitive experience but also of the behavior appropriate to such an educational experience. Duties will be performed fairly, efficiently, and without drawing undue attention to the official. In order to strengthen the official's effectiveness, personal evaluation of performance will be made and solicitation of constructive criticism from coaches, players, and administrators will be sought. Though receiving a fee, the ultimate reward to the official will be that of having rendered a valuable service to girls and women who have found personal meaning in expressing themselves through the medium of sport.

Standards for Officials' Ratings

Note: Changes from the previous *Guide* have been indicated by underlining.

I. Basketball, Competitive Swimming and Diving, Soccer, Softball (Fast Pitch and Slow Pitch), Track-Field, and Volleyball.

There are six ratings for officials, five of which qualify the holder to officiate sports contests. Each is designed to meet the needs of various sports events and to stimulate interest of individuals who desire to officiate.

The *Examiner's rating* signifies the holder is qualified to rate officials. This rating does not certify the holder to officiate sports contests.

The *Intramural rating* qualifies the holder to officiate contests in the school in which the holder is enrolled or contests of comparable level.

The *Apprentice rating* qualifies the holder to officiate contests which may be adequately controlled by a competent, but inexperienced official.

The *Local rating* signifies that the holder is qualified to officiate interscholastic and intercollegiate contests requiring a competent and experienced official.

The *State rating* signifies that the holder is capable of officiating any contest within the state or region where the rating is awarded.

The *National rating* signifies that the holder is capable of officiating any contest anywhere in the United States. This rating is for the most highly skilled official.

All ABO officials are required to take the theoretical examination yearly. Specific requirements for all ratings are outlined below.

Examiner

1. Prerequisite — must have held a state or national rating for a minimum period of six years. (The six years need not be consecutive but must be within the previous eight-year period.)
2. Theoretical examination[1] — national examination, minimum 82.
3. Duration— two years from next June 1.
4. Renewal:
   a. In order to be eligible for renewal, the candidate must have been involved in the rating or training of officials.

---

[1] Form A and Form B of the ABO Theoretical Examinations *must* be administered as closed book examinations.

b. To renew, the candidate must pass the national theoretical examination with a minimum score of 82.
c. Should the rating lapse for one year or less, the candidate remains eligible for renewal.
d. Should the ratings lapse for more than one year, the candidate must qualify through earning a State rating.
5. This rating is transferable to other Boards.

Intramural Official

1. Minimum standards — set by Affiliated Board.
2. Duration — two years from next June 1.

Apprentice Official

1. Minimum standards can be set by the affiliated board, or these standards may be followed:
   a. Theoretical examination[1] — national examination, minimum 60.
   b. Practical examination[2] — minimum 75; minimum number of raters: at least one rater with a local rating or above.
2. Duration —two years from next June 1.

Local Official

1. Theoretical examination[1] — national examination, minimum 76.
2. Practical examination[2]—minimum 80; minimum number of raters: two raters; one rater must have a local rating or above.
3. Duration — two years from next June 1.
4. This rating is transferable to other Boards.

State Official

1. Theoretical examination[1] — national examination, minimum 82.
2. Practical examination[2]—minimum 85; minimum number of raters: three raters; one rater must have a state rating; others must be local or above.
3. Duration — two years from next June 1.
4. This rating is transferable to other Boards.

---

[2]Any rating team may include no more than one Examiner and no more than one Honorary National. See Alternate Practical Rating Procedures and Methods for Practical Renewal in this section.

National Official

Note: National Ratings for Basketball and Volleyball can only be awarded by ABO National Rating Teams.

1. Theoretical examination[1]—national examination, minimum 88.
2. Practical examination[2]—minimum 88; minimum number of raters: three raters; one rater must have a national or honorary national; others must be local or above.
3. Duration — two years from next June 1.
4. This rating is transferable to other Boards.

National Official in Basketball and Volleyball

An official must apply to attend a national rating session. The following criteria must be met for an official to apply:

a. Must have officiated with a current State rating for 2 years, or have officiated with a current National rating, or have officiated with an Honorary National rating.

b. Must have passed the written test scoring 88 or above, administered and verified by the local officiating board chair.

c. Must have officiated at a national, state, regional, or qualifying tournament in at least 1 of the 2 previous years; *OR* must have obtained signatures of three (3) *different* individuals who serve in any of the following capacities:

   (1) basketball or volleyball, college or university Women's coach (2 maximum)
   (2) volleyball or basketball National Rating Team member (1 maximum)
   (3) certifying Board Chair
   (4) NAGWS National official with National Tournament officiating experience
   (5) officiating coordinator or tournament director of a national, state, regional, or qualifying women's basketball or volleyball tournament (1 maximum)

A national basketball rating is valid for 3 years from next June 1. A national volleyball rating is valid for 4 years from next June 1. Both ratings are transferable to other boards.

For additional information write to: the National Rating Team Coordinator (NRT)

Basketball:
Margie Wright
904 Green Ave.
Normal, IL 61761

Volleyball:
Ann Casey
12300 SW Douglas
Portland, OR 97225

Application forms are available from the NAGWS National Office and your local board chair.

II. Gymnastics

Class I Official

1. Minimum grade[3]—theoretical (optional) and practical: 80%; 85% average; compulsory: 85%
2. Eligibility—20 years of age; must have previously attained a State, Regional, or National rating
3. Duration—ur til December, 1984 (throughout the Olympiad)
4. Examinatio.: content
   Practical—optional exercises in all four events
   Theoretical—50 questions Class I Compulsories and 50 optional questions
5. Qualified to judge any Class I competition in any geographical area
6. Must maintain active status by fulfilling all requirements on the Active Status Report forms.

Class II Official

1. Minimum grade[3]—theoretical (optional) and practical: 70%; 75% average; compulsory: 70%
2. Eligibility—18 years of age; must have previously attained a minimum of Apprentice rating
3. Duration—until December, 1984 (throughout the Olympiad)
4. Examination content
   Practical—optional exercises in all four events
   Theoretical—50 questions Class II Compulsories and 50 optional questions
5. Qualified to judge Class II competitions up to and including the state level in any geographical area; must maintain active status at Class II for one year before being eligible to take the Class I rating examination.
6. Must maintain active status by fulfilling all requirements on the Active Status Report forms.

Class III Official

1. Minimum grade[3]—theoretical (optional): 70%; 70% average; compulsory: 65%
2. Eligibility—16 years of age
3. Duration—until December, 1984 (throughout the Olympiad)

---

[3]Minimum % score for both theoretical and practical examinations must be met as stated. In the event the practical examination is not required, theoretical minimum scores apply.

4. Examination content
   Practical—optional exercises in all four events
   Theoretical—50 questions on Class III compulsories and 50 optional questions
5. Qualified to judge any Class III meet in any geographical area; must maintain active status at Class III for one certification year before being eligible to take the Class II examination.

Class IV Official

The requirements for obtaining a Class IV rating are the same as those for Class III with the following exceptions:
1. Minimum grade—theoretical only: 70%
2. Examination content—theoretical examination consisting of 40 questions on Class IV compulsories and 10 questions on general knowledge.
3. Qualified to judge any class IV meet in any geographical area.

III. Synchronized Swimming

There are 3 ratings for officials of Synchronized Swimming. Each is designed to meet the needs of various types of events and to stimulate the interest of individuals who desire to officiate.

The *Local* rating signifies that the holder is qualified to officiate interscholastic and intercollegiate contests requiring a competent and experienced official.

The *Regional* rating signifies that the holder is capable of officiating any contest within the state or region where the rating is awarded.

The *National* rating signifies that the holder is capable of officiating any contest anywhere in the United States. This rating is for the most highly skilled official.

Specific requirements for all ratings are outlined below.

Local Official

1. Theoretical examination[1]—national examination, minimum 76.
2. Practical examination[4]—minimum 80.
3. Duration—two years from next June 1.
4. This rating is transferable to other Boards.

---

[4]Practical examinations are taken by viewing and evaluating a film. For more specific information, contact the ABO Synchronized Swimming E and R Chairperson.

Regional Official

1. Theoretical examination[1]—national examination, minimum 82.
2. Practical examination[4]—minimum 85.
3. Duration—two years from next June 1.
4. This rating is transferable to other Boards.

National Official

1. Theoretical examination[1]—national examination, minimum 88.
2. Practical examination[4]—minimum 88.
3. Duration—two years from next June 1.
4. This rating is transferable to other Boards.

Alternative Methods for Practical Examinations

A. New Candidates

1. New NAGWS/ABO candidates (inexperienced or unregistered) can qualify for an apprentice rating by meeting one of the following criteria:
   a. attend a series of structured clinics set up by the Board, the number to be specified by the Board, *or*
   b. secure a passing grade and the recommendation of the instructor in an officiating course at the college level (the course must be approved by the Board), *or*
   c. attend officiating courses offered by another organization. Candidate must secure a recommendation from said course and such a course must be approved by the Board. Courses offered by recreation departments or adult education would be acceptable.

   New apprentices shall work with more experienced officials for a number of contests, as designated by the affiliated board.

2. New NAGWS/ABO candidates (those who are experienced officials and/or registered with other officiating organizations) can be awarded a rating after completing the following requirements:
   a. receiving the appropriate score on the NAGWS/ABO Theoretical Examination (Form A or Form B); and,
   b. demonstrating ability to use ABO officiating techniques. The local Affiliated Board shall specify the nature of the demonstration but shall recognize the official's experience.

B. Methods for Practical Renewal

1. An official may renew or *upgrade* a rating by officiating under observation of the examining committee. See this section for number of raters required.

2. Alternative Method for Renewing at the *same level:* (Exception: basketball and volleyball nationals, gymnastics officials, and synchronized swimming officials.)

   a. officiate a minimum of 3 intercollegiate, interscholastic, or interagency contests during which a minimum of 5 different evaluators are involved. Evaluations may be sought from coaches of the teams involved and/or ABO officials watching the contest. (The NAGWS/ABO official must have a rating comparable to that being sought by the renewal candidate.) Prior to the contest, the candidate shall ask the coaches and/or officials to respond on the evaluation postcard[5] addressed to the appropriate sports chair, indicating the quality of officiating. After the contest, the person responding should fill out the postcard, indicating an opinion as to the competency of the official and mail it to the appropriate sports chair. If an average of 4 is scored by the official as indicated from the 5 responses, a national rating is automatic, providing that a minimum of 88 had been scored on the theoretical examination. If an average of 3.5 is scored by the official as indicated from the 5 responses, a state rating is automatic, providing that a minimum of 82 had been scored on the written examination.

   b. officiate a designated number of contests, such to be designated by the board.

If written complaints are received about an official renewing as in a. or b. above, a more formal method should be used.

Patch and Uniform

All NAGWS/ABO officials are required to wear an official ABO patch which can be purchased, *only* by board chairs, from the National Office. Patches are sport and rating specific, i.e., Regional, Synchronized Swimming.

The following uniform is required of all ABO officials receiving fees for their services:

Shirt—Navy blue and white alternating stripes

---

[5] See current *ABO Directory /Handbook* for sample evaluation form.

Jacket—Navy blue
Pants /Shorts—Navy blue
Kilt—Navy blue
Shoes—All white leather (exceptions: softball—black, soccer—black)
Socks—White (exception: softball—navy blue)
Belt—Navy blue

Note: Local Boards are encouraged to adopt uniform regulations for each contest such that each official is easily identifiable. For safety reasons, both officials should be attired the same.

Manufacturers will attach the standard NAGWS/ABO label to indicate that the item has been approved (sample tag shown below). For a list of approved manufacturers and distributors, contact the NAGWS National Office.

Made to the
Specifications of
NAGWS/ABO

Official Uniform for National Officials Rated by the Volleyball or Basketball NRT's

Volleyball: Navy blue and white striped shirt approved by NAGWS/ABO; navy blue dress slacks (skirts or culottes are not acceptable); completely white socks; all white and clean shoes; no jacket.

Basketball: Navy blue and white striped shirt approved by NAGWS/ABO; navy blue dress slacks or skirt, culottes, kilt (length shall be between knee and mid-thigh); completely white crew socks; white shoes; navy blue blazer or jacket may be worn (sweaters and warm-ups may not be worn).

Note: When officiating within a local area, a National Official may have to adjust this uniform slightly to ensure easy identification within a sport contest. For regional or national championships this uniform will be expected, however.

Recommended Fees

Local boards should establish fees that reflect the level of rating of the official as well as the type and level of competition within their locale. Boards are encouraged to establish fees in conjunction with local governing groups. The fee schedule should reflect differential pay based upon rating levels.

It is strongly recommended that fee schedules not differ from that of officials of boys' sports, given substantially similar type and level of competition as girls' sports.

Registration of Officials

Most states require those who officiate either boys' or girls' interscholastic contests to be registered with the State High School Athletic Association or other administrative body. All NAGWS/ABO officials who officiate high school or junior high school games are urged to cooperate fully with their state regulatory body.

Amateur Standing of Officials

An official who wishes to maintain amateur status as a participant in a sport must be aware of the ruling(s) on amateur status established by various governing bodies for that sport.

Amateur status is defined by high school and college governing bodies as well as by national sport governing bodies that hold the franchise from international sport governing groups.

The official who wishes to maintain amateur status as a participant is responsible for investigating the specific regulations of *each* governing body with jurisdiction over such eligibility.

National Governing Bodies

Basketball—Write the Amateur Basketball Association of the United States of America, 1750 E. Boulder St., Colorado Springs, CO 80909.

Competitive Diving—Write U.S. Diving Inc., P.O. Box 1811, Indianapolis, IN 46206.

Competitive Swimming—Write U.S. Swimming, 3400 W. 86th St., Indianapolis, IN 46268.

Gymnastics—Write the United States Gymnastics Federation, P.O. Box 7686, Fort Worth, TX 76111.

Soccer—Write the United States Soccer Federation, 350 Fifth Ave., Suite 4010, New York, NY 10001.

Softball (Fast Pitch and Slow Pitch)—Write Amateur Softball Association, 2801 N.E. 50th St., P.O. Box 11437, Oklahoma City, OK 73111.

Synchronized Swimming—Write U.S. Synchronized Swimming Inc., 1750 E. Boulder, Colorado Springs, CO 80909.

Track and Field—Write the Athletic Congress, 3400 W. 86th St., Indianapolis, IN 46268.

Volleyball—Write the United States Volleyball Association, 1750 E. Boulder St., Colorado Springs, CO 80909.

How to Become a Rated Official

1. Study the rules, the article on the techniques of officiating, and the study questions.
2. Attend interpretations meetings and officiating clinics or training courses conducted in your vicinity.
3. Practice often. To some, officiating comes easily; to others it comes only as the result of hard work and concentration. Welcome criticism and work hard to improve.
4. Find out from the chair of the nearest affiliated board when examinations for ratings are to be held. (Consult list of boards in ABO Directory/Handbook available from NAGWS/AAHPERD, 1900 Association Drive, Reston, VA 22091. **Cost:** $3.00.)
5. Take your rating remembering that it is the aim of the Affiliated Boards of Officials to maintain high standards for officials.

Information for Affiliated Boards

How to Establish a Board of Officials

1. Establish the need for an affiliated board by contacting individuals in the area who have current ratings or who are interested in standardizing and raising the level of officiating basketball, competitive swimming and diving, gymnastics, soccer, softball (fast pitch and slow pitch), synchronized swimming, track and field, or volleyball in that area.
2. Write to ABO Past Chair, c/o NAGWS/AAHPERD, 1900 Association Drive, Reston, VA 22091, for a sample copy of an authorized constitution for officials' boards and application for becoming an affiliated board.
3. At a designated meeting of interested individuals present plans for forming a board.
   a. choose a name which will permit expansion of function as need may arise; do not limit title to one sport.

b. from the group, elect a chair, chair-elect, secretary, and treasurer.

c. form an examining committee of at least three members for each sport in which you would like to give ratings. If any member has been rated elsewhere, such experience should be helpful; such a rating is not necessary, however. It is suggested that members of the examining committee be examined and obtain ratings from other affiliated boards whenever possible.

d. make plans for drawing up a constitution according to the sample copy received from the NAGWS/ABO Program Administrator. Plan to devote some time to the study of the rules and to practice officiating. If possible, secure the assistance of some rated official in each sport for which the Board anticipates giving ratings.

4. Send the completed application form, two copies of the local constitution, and a check for $25 non-refundable affiliation fee (made payable to the NAGWS Affiliated Boards of Officials) to the NAGWS/ABO Program Administrator. Indicate the sports in which you wish to grant ratings by listing the names and qualifications of *3* interested individuals. Approval of the application will come from the ABO Past Chair who will request that examination packets be sent to your Affiliated Board Chair for all sports in which your Board is authorized to give ratings. At this time, you will also receive a current copy of the *ABO Directory/Handbook*. The process of accepting an application for affiliation of a new Board and of requesting that the proper examination packets be sent ordinarily takes several weeks. Prospective Boards, therefore, should file for affiliation at least 2 months before they wish to hold rating sessions.

5. Administer Form A of the National Theoretical Examination. Form B of the National Theoretical Examination may be administered to those who did not pass Form A. The Intramural Examination may be given as a practice test to those candidates pursuing ratings.

6. To cover expenses involved in reproduction and evaluation of written examinations, boards may charge a fee each time an individual takes a written examination.

7. Conduct practice sessions in rating officials. All persons on the examining committee who have not previously rated officials should have a minimum of three practice sessions prior to actually rating. Secure the assistance of a rated official in these practice sessions if at all possible.

8. Give practical examinations to individuals who pass the written examination. (Note minimum number of raters required to give various ratings, in this section.)
9. Order appropriate rating cards and patches from the NAGWS National Office for distribution to those who pass the theoretical and practical examination.
10. Send lists of approved officials to schools and other organizations in the area. This notice should indicate the fees for officiating and should give the name, address, rating, and telephone number of each official.
11. Keep accurate lists of all persons receiving ratings. In these sports in which your Board was authorized to give ratings forward these lists to the NAGWS/ABO Program Administrator. An appropriate form is included in each examination packet. Due date for submitting all forms: **June 1**; exception: Gymnastics due March 1. Send completed exam answer sheets to the E & R Chair, who conducts a yearly item analysis.

Adding Sports—Expansion of Services

Should a Board wish to add ratings in other sports, the Chair of the Board should write the NAGWS/ABO Program Administrator c/o NAGWS National Office. The Board should indicate the names of a minimum of 3 persons qualified to act as examiners in that sport for the next 2 years. Qualifications and experience in the sport should be listed for each potential examiner. Should your Board qualify, you will be notified by the ABO Past Chair and will receive a packet for administering examinations.

Maintaining Affiliated Status

To maintain affiliated status in each sport in which it gives ratings, a Board must:

1. Pay dues each year to the NAGWS National Office. (Notification will be sent each Fall.) Beginning with the 1984-85 school year dues must be submitted with the yearly report, on or before June 1.
2. Submit a yearly sport report to the NAGWS National Office regarding the current status of rated officials. (Reports for each sport must be submitted by **June 1,** with the exception of Gymnastics, which is due by January 1. Appropriate forms are included in examination packets.)

Note: Examination packets are mailed yearly to *qualified* boards on:
   April 1—Soccer
   July 1—Volleyball
   August 1—Basketball

September 15—Competitive Swimming and Diving
October 15—Track & Field
January 1—Gymnastics
January 30—Synchronized Swimming
February 1—Fast Pitch Softball & Slow Pitch Softball

If you do not receive your packet(s) within two weeks of the above dates, contact the NAGWS/ABO Program Administrator, 1900 Association Dr., Reston, VA 22091. (703) 476-3451

All information for boards may be found in the current *ABO Directory /Handbook* which may be purchasef for $3.00 from NAGWS, 1900 Association Dr., Reston, VA 22091. (703) 476-3450.

Track and Field Study Questions 1983-85

Running Events

Directions: Read all questions carefully. Select the *one* item which best answers each question.

1. In a preliminary heat of the 800 meter run, Susan accidentally bumps into Mary causing her to trip and fall. Mary gets up and finishes the race. What is the official decision?
   A. Heat stands as run.
   B. Heat is rerun.
   C. Susan is disqualified and heat results then stand.
   D. Susan is disqualified and the referee may allow Mary to run in semi-finals.

2. How many individuals should be taken to the finals in the 800 meter run on a six lane track?
   A. 6   B. 8   C. 10   D. 12

3. In the absence of a Games Committee, which official must rule on late entries and substitutions?
   A. Clerk of course.
   B. Meet director.
   C. Meet referee.
   D. Scorer.

4. What is the official's decision when a runner is lapped during a race?
   A. Disqualify runner.
   B. Legal, runner continues.
   C. Tell lapped runner to leave the track.
   D. Tell lapped runner to move out to the third lane.

5. The runners in lanes 1 and 3 each have one false start. As the group assumes the "Set" position, runners in lanes 1, 2 and 3 roll out just before the gun is fired. What should the starter do?
   A. Warn all three runners.
   B. Charge runner in lane 2 with a false start.
   C. Disqualify runners in lane 1 and 3, charge 2 with a false start.
   D. Charge runner in lane 2 with a false start and disqualify runners.

6. The time for the first place in the 100 meter hurdles is :14.6; the time for second place is :14.5, with the time for third place: 14.8 What is the official second place time?

   A. :14.6
   B. :14.7
   C. :14.65
   D. No time is recorded.

7. As Runner A is passing to Runner B, the baton is dropped. The baton lands on the infield of the track. What is the official's decision?

   A. Legal, if Runner A picks the baton up and does not interfere with the other runners.
   B. Legal, if Runner B picks the baton up and does not interfere with the other runners.
   C. Legal, if either of the runners pick the baton up as long as they do not interfere with the other runners.
   D. They are immediately disqualified.

8. Which of the following is the correct event for the heptathlon?

   A. 100 meter, hurdles, shot put, high jump, 200 meter dash, long jump, javelin, 800 meter run.
   B. 400 meter, hurdles, high jump, 800 meter run, shot put, long jump, 200 meter dash, javelin.
   C. 1500 meter run, shot put, high jump, javelin, long jump, 100 meter hurdles, 200 meter dash.
   D. 200 meter dash, long jump, high jump, shot put, discus, 100 meter hurdles, 800 meter run.

9. In cross-country running, what does a blue flag indicate about the course being followed?

   A. Danger ahead.
   B. Right turn.
   C. Left turn.
   D. Course continues straight ahead.

10. In computing total team scores, if two or more teams have identical scores, what is the procedure?

   A. The team with the individual competitor scoring the most points is declared the winner.
   B. The team placing the highest in the last event of the competition is declared the winner.
   C. The team scoring the greatest number of first places is declared the winner.
   D. The teams are declared co-winners of the meet.

11. In races in which runners are not required to remain in lanes when may a runner cross in front of another runner?
    A. When the runner will not impede the progress of another runner.
    B. When the runner is one running stride ahead of the other.
    C. When the runner is two running strides ahead of the other.
    D. When the runner is three running strides ahead of the other.
12. Which is *not true* in indoor track competition?
    A. 400 meter relay will not use an international zone.
    B. 1600 meter relay will be run with a two-turn stagger.
    C. 25 competitors are declared for the 5000 meter runs; therefore, sections are run.
    D. 16 competitors are declared for the 1000 meter run; therefore, only one final heat will be required.
13. A hurdler deliberately knocks down several hurdles during a race. What is the referee's decision?
    A. This is legal.
    B. The hurdler is warned.
    C. The race should be rerun.
    D. The hurdler is immediately disqualified from the event.
14. A competitor reports for the start of the 100 meter dash finals as the starting gun is being fired. What should the starter do?
    A. Recall the runners.
    B. Let the race continue.
    C. Allow the runner to run alone.
    D. Recall runners and penalize the late competitor.
15. Which of the following is *not* a violation in race walking?
    A. Race walker maintains contact with the ground.
    B. Race walker does not fully extend the leg.
    C. Race walker does not maintain contact with the ground.
    D. Race walker does not have the supporting leg in a vertically upright position.
16. In the combined events competition, how many attempts does the competitor get in the shot put and the long jump?
    A. Three attempts.
    B. Three attempts in preliminaries and three in the finals if the competitor qualifies.
    C. Four attempts.
    D. Six attempts.
17. What distances should be marked on a 5000 meter cross-country course?
    A. ½ mile, 1 mile, 1½ mile, 2 mile, 2½ mile, and 3 mile points.
    B. Mile, two mile and three mile.

C. 800, 1600, 2400, 3200, 4000, 4800 meter points.

D. 1600, 3200 and 4800 meter points.

18. The first place watches read 24.4, 23.9, 23.5 in the 200 meter dash. What is the official time for first place?

A. 23.5

B. 23.9

C. 23.8

D. 24.2

19. A pentathlon competitor makes two false starts. What is the proper procedure?

A. She is allowed one more attempt.

B. She must be replaced by another runner.

C. She is warned and moved two strides behind other runners.

D. She is disqualified.

20. In the pentathlon, the 100 meter hurdles was fully automatically timed, during the 800 meter run the FAT system failed. What should the track referee rule?

A. Use FAT times for 100 hurdles, hand times for 800 meter run.

B. Use hand times for both 100 hurdles and 800 meter dash.

C. Convert the 800 meter hand timer to FAT times and use 100 meter hurdles.

D. Convert the 100 hurdles FAT times to hand times and use 800 meter hand times.

21. How much time should be allowed between rounds of competition?

A. 20 minutes for 100 meter dash.

B. 45 minutes for 400 meter dash.

C. 90 minutes for 2 mile run.

D. Three hours for 2 mile run.

22. On a cross-country course, the first turn should be located how far from the starting line?

A. Between 30-40 yards.

B. Between 75-100 yards.

C. Between 330-440 yards.

D. Between 440-880 yards.

23. In preliminary rounds for running events, a minimum of how many competitors from each heat should go to the next round?

A. 1   B. 2   C. 3   D. 4

24. How many points are given for relays in a dual meet in which each team may enter three competitors?

A. 5 for first; 2 for second.

B. 5 for first; 1 for second.

C. 5 for first; 0 for second.

D. 7 for first; 3 for second.

25. Split times for the 3000 meters run should be given:
   A. Each time the runners pass the finish line.
   B. Each time the runners pass the 3000 meter starting line.
   C. Each time the runners complete the 1500 meters.
   D. Splits are not given during the 3000 meter race.

Field Events

1. Who must give permission for a shot put competitor to use tape on a hand to cover a wound?
   A. Official doctor.
   B. Meet Director.
   C. Official certified trainer.
   D. Games Committee.
2. After other competitors have been disqualified from the high jump how long may the one remaining jumper continue to compete?
   A. Until she has three consecutive unsuccessful attempts.
   B. As long as the competitor wishes.
   C. For 15 minutes following the failure of the last competitor.
   D. Until she has two consecutive unsuccessful attempts.
3. Which method is correct in measuring the shot put?
   A. From the outside edge of the stop-board to the nearest mark made by the fall of the shot.
   B. From the inside edge of the stop-board to the nearest mark made by the fall of the shot.
   C. From the nearest mark made by the fall of the shot to the outside circumference on a lone through the center of the circle.
   D. From the nearest mark made by the fall of the shot to the inside circumference of the circle on a line through the center of the circle.
4. In the discus throw, which of the following is not a foul?
   A. Touching the ground outside the circle prior to the discus being marked.
   B. Falling down inside the circle after throwing the discus.
   C. Leaving the circle from the front after the discus has been marked.
   D. The discus landing on a sector line.
5. To watch for the fouls in the high jump, where should the head field judge stand?
   A. To the side of the performer in a position to observe the plane of the bar to the ground.
   B. In line with the performer's take-off spot to observe the plane of the bar to the ground.

C. Behind one of the jumping standards to observe the plane of the bar to the ground.

D. Beside one of the jumping standards in a position to observe the plane of the bar to the ground.

6. Which of the following is a violation of the rules in the high jump?
   A. Using an approach which is greater than 15 meters.
   B. Placing marks in the runway to aid the jumper in the approach.
   C. Placing an object on the crossbar to assist the jumper in focusing for the jump.
   D. Using a two foot take-off.

7. The exact measurement of the long jump is 5.486 meters. How should the jump be officially recorded?
   A. 5.0
   B. 5.4
   C. 5.48
   D. 5.49

8. Below are the results of four high jump competitors; which jumper would be declared third place?

	4'8''	4'10''	5'	5'1''	5'2''	5'3''	5'4''
1.	...	...	√	x √	xx √	xxx	
2.	...	√	x	x √	xx √	xxx	
3.	...	...	√	√	x √	xx √	√
4.	x	√		√	√	xx √	xxx

   A. Tie between 1 and 2.
   B. Tie between 2 and 3.
   C. 2
   D. 1

9. On levels of competition other than intercollegiate, how is the number of events in which an individual can participate determined?
   A. By the host school.
   B. By the Games Committee.
   C. By the coaches involved.
   D. By the State or local governing body.

10. After throwing the javelin, the competitor hops on one foot to maintain balance and steps on one of the runway lines. What is the proper decision?
    A. Throw does not count as a trial.
    B. Legal throw; measurement is taken.
    C. Foul; trial counts but is not measured.
    D. Foul; one more trial permitted.

11. When should measurements of throws be recorded to the nearest centimeter below the distance covered?
    A. All shot put measurements.
    B. Throws above 35 meters.
    C. Discus throws below 30 meters.
    D. Javelin throws below 30 meters.
12. During the preliminary competition, a coach tells her long jumper how they should change their approach. What is the procedure?
    A. This is legal; competition continues.
    B. The coach is warned by the referee.
    C. The competitor is credited with one foul jump.
    D. The competitor is immediately disqualified from the competition.
13. When are impounded discuses returned to the competitors?
    A. At the conclusion of the preliminaries.
    B. At the conclusion of the finals.
    C. When the competitor completes the third throw in the preliminaries.
    D. When it is discovered it does not weigh the correct amount.
14. Lanes in the final round of competition shall be formed under the direction of which official?
    A. Meet Director.
    B. Games Committee.
    C. Clerk of course.
    D. Track Referee.
15. If a suitable warmup area is available, how many throws will the softball throw judge allow each competitor to take before the competition begins?
    A. As many as the competitor can get in from the first call until the event starts.
    B. Two throws under the supervision of field event judges.
    C. Three throws under the supervision of field event judges.
    D. Four throws under the supervision of field event judges.
16. When a record is set in the long jump, who must approve the measurement?
    A. The field referee and two field judges.
    B. The long jump field judge.
    C. The Games Committee.
    D. The Meet Director.
17. The winner of the heptathlon in a meet where six teams are present will score how many points for her team?
    A. 20.

B. 10
C. 5
D. 0

18. What is the first step in resolving a tie in the high jump?
    A. Jumper with lowest number of total misses wins.
    B. Jumper with the lowest number of trials wins.
    C. Ties remain, jumpers divide points as in other events.
    D. Jumper with the lowest number of trials at which the height at which the tie occurred wins.

19. How is the order of competition in the finals of the throwing events determined?
    A. The best performer in the preliminaries competes first in the finals.
    B. The best performer in the preliminaries competes last in the finals.
    C. The competitors are placed in throwing order by random draw.

20. The following performances occurred during the discus. What is the correct finishing position of these competitors?

	A	B	C	D
Qualifying	19'5''	19'6''	Foul	18'10''
Round	18'6''	18'5''	21'6''	18'4½''
	18'5''	21'7''	19'6''	19'2''
Preliminaries	Foul	19'6''	19'10''	18'10½''
	18'10''	19'6''	20'5''	19'4''
	18'10½''	18'3''	19'10''	19'4''
Finals	Foul	18'5''	18'6''	19'1''
	18'3''	19'6''	18'8''	19'4''
	19'4''	19'7½''	18'3''	18'5''

    A. C, B, D, A
    B. B, C, Tie for Third A and D
    C. C, B, A, D
    D. B, C, D, A

21. In a meet with four teams, each team being allowed to enter two individuals per team, how many points are given for first place?
    A. 5   B. 6   C. 7   D. 10

22. Two high jumpers remain tied for 1st place after all of the normal tie breaking procedures have been used. What is the official's next procedure he should follow?
    A. Tie remains.
    B. The two jumpers jump once more at the height at which the tie occurred.

C. Jumpers flip a coin for points and ribbon.

D. Jumper which began jumping first wins.

23. The following individuals have been randomly drawn for competition in the discus throw: B, F, G, H, A, C, I, D, J, E, K, L, and N. Which of the following reflects proper draw?

A. Flight 1: B, F, G, H, A, C, I
Flight 2: D, J, E, K, L, N

B. Flight 1: B, J, A, I, J, K, N
Flight 2: F, H, C, D, E, L

C. Flight 1: B, H, A, D, J, L, N
Flight 2: F, G, C, I, E, K

D. Flight 1: B, F, G, I, D, J
Flight 2: H, A, C, E, K, L, N

24. A discus thrower begins her throw, stops, lays her discus down in the circle, and leaves the back of the circle. She wipes her hands off. She re-enters the back of the circle and finishes her throw. The entire process takes 60 seconds. What is the decision of the official?

A. Legal.

B. Foul, illegal to leave circle.

C. Foul, time was too great.

D. Foul, to lay down the implement.

25. During the high jump competition, a competitor leaves to run in the 200 meter dash. Upon completion of the dash she immediately returns, the bar has been raised two inches. The official is preparing to raise it another two inches. What is the decision of the official?

A. If the competitor has immediately returned from the running event, give her time to recover (maximum of ten minutes.) Allow her to jump at the height bar is at upon her return.

B. Raise the bar, the competitor must compete at the new height.

C. Lower the bar two inches to allow her to jump at the height of when she left.

D. Competitor is disqualified for leaving the site of the event.

Answers and Rule References

Running Events

1. D 5:3q
2. A 5:2a (2)
3. B PTO III:2b (1)
4. B 5:4f
5. C 5:3k
6. D PTO VI:6k
7. C 5:6b (12)
8. D 8:5
9. D 9:1i
10. C 2:2b
11. A 5:3n, 3p
12. D 7:3,4
13. D 5:5c (1)
14. B 4:12
15. A 5:7a
16. A 8:6e
17. C 9:1f
18. D PTO VI:6j (1)
19. A 8:6e
20. B 8:6d
21. D 5:2b
22. C 9:1f
23. B 5:2b
24. C 2:1a
25. B 5:4c

Field Events

1. A 6:61
2. A 6:3b
3. D 6:7b (5); PTO VII, 2S (1)
4. B 6:8b (2)

5. D PTO VII, 2 1(5)
6. D 6:3a (8); 6:3b (7,8)
7. C 6:1d; 6:2d
8. A 6:3b (15)
9. D 4:4
10. C 6:9b (4e)
11. A 6:1d
12. B 4:14
13. B PTOV, 5b
14. D PTO VI 1c
15. C 6:1j
16. A 10:2f
17. B 2:1f
18. B 6:3b (15a)
19. C 6:1a
20. A 2:1c; 6:11
21. B 2:1a
22. B 6:3 (15d)
23. C 6:1b (1), PTO VII:1l (1)
24. A 6:6g
25. A 6:3b (11, 13, 16)

Principles and Techniques of Officiating Track and Field

Revised by the ABO Principles and Techniques of Officiating Committee

I. Desirable Qualities for Making A Good Official

Officiating track and field events demands much more than just knowing and interpreting the rules. Listed below are some of the qualities desirable in a good official.

1. Each official should be familiar with the track and field rules as outlined in the current *NAGWS Track and Field Guide*. However, when a violation occurs which is not covered definitely in the rules, the official should reflect the spirit of fair play and apply decisions as objectively as possible.
2. Being a good official demands something more than just performing the duties listed in the *Guide*. A decisive personality is desirable; an official must be able to make prompt, immediate and accurate decisions on many complex questions.
3. In the excitement of competition many unfortunate incidents can occur to spoil the meet. An official must be able to anticipate such incidents and, with a timely warning or firm action, prevent a good meet from being marred.
4. The official should be courteous, just, accurate, and objective at all times.
5. Being a good judge of track and field events demands the ability to concentrate on the immediate task. Often several events are scheduled simultaneously, and it is therefore easy for one's attention to stray from one event to another.

II. Suggested Officials for a Meet

The number of officials necessary to conduct a meet varies. Dual meets will not require as many officials as larger meets. For maximum efficiency, the following officials are suggested for meets where three or more places are being awarded:

1 meet director

1 track referee

1 field referee

1 clerk of course

1 starter

7 finish judges, including chief

7 timers, including chief

6 inspectors

1 custodian of awards

1 lap counter

fully automatic timing officials

1 custodian of equipment

1 marshal

1 scorer

1 announcer

1 surveyor

1 recorder if new records made

3 field judges per event, including chief

1 wind gauge operator

If necessary, assistants may be provided for all of the above. No official should act in a dual capacity, nor should any track team or club team manager act as an official at a track and field championship meet.

III. Procedures and Techniques of Officiating

1. General Procedures

a. An official should be sure of date, time and place when accepting an assignment.

b. If unable to keep an appointment, an official should notify the meet director at least 24 hours in advance.

c. An official should arrive at the track 30 minutes before the meet is scheduled to start.

d. An official should wear the official NAGWS-ABO uniform or other appropriate identifying attire designated for the meet.

e. An official should make introductions to the meet director, track and field referees and other officials.

f. An official should get the assignment from the meet director and report to the person in charge of the event. The official in charge of an event should check off other officials as they report in.

2. Procedures and Techniques of Meet Officials

a. Games Committee

1. shall have the responsibility for meet conduct and shall give special assistance to the meet director.

2. shall have jurisdiction of all matters relative to the competition.

3. shall serve as a jury of appeals and consultants to rule on all questions of the meet director and referee(s).

4. shall have the authority to cancel or postpone any event if the competition cannot be conducted or completed in a satisfactory manner.

5. shall determine the order of events, if not standard, and rule on all changes in the published order.
6. shall approve the forming of the heats and number of qualifiers as proposed by the referee(s).
7. shall make changes in the placing of competition in any field or running event if the conditions are so justified.
8. shall generally consist of the following members: a chairperson, a rules interpreter, an ABO official representative, a coaches representative and an at-large member. (For national competition, members of the NAGWS Rules Committee may serve on the Games Committee.)
9. shall rule on all late entries, substitutions, and protests submitted under the provisions of Rule 3.

b. Meet Director
1. shall (in the absence of a games committee):
   - have the responsibilities of the organization and conduct of the meet.
   - determine the order and number of events. In other than intercollegiate meets, the number of entries per event may be restricted due to facilities and time.
   - rule upon all late entries or substitutions.
2. shall designate numbers to be used at the meet. It is suggested the numbers be $1' \times 5\frac{1}{4}''$. Four safety pins should be included to assure they stay on the uniform.
3. shall obtain all the equipment necessary for all officials and for the running of the meet.
4. shall be directly responsible for the procuring of the track itself and securing all the officials necessary for the running of the meet.
5. shall send out the entry forms and meet information and be the recipient of the entry forms when they are returned.
6. shall arrange for the coaches and officials meeting prior to the meet, if scheduled.
7. shall establish standards for qualifying for the high jump:
   - In large meets of two or three days of championship meets, when the number of entries is so large as to prevent optimum competitive conditions, a qualifying standard must be established in order that the field be cut to 12-15 competitors.
   - The easiest and most often utilized method involves listing the jumpers in descending order according to the best performance during the current season. Count down from the best performance approximately five (5) past the

number who are to be qualified and set the Qualifying Height at that mark. Example: if 12 are desired for the finals, count down through the 17th performer and take that mark rounding to the nearest inch.

- The opening height for the qualifying round should be 4″ (10cm) less than the standard for qualifying to the finals. The bar then should be raised 2″ (5cm) after the first jumps, and then by 1″ (3cm) increments until the qualifying height is reached. When during the warmup period, the opening height proves to be too stringent for *all* competitors this should be reported to the meet director who should take appropriate action by lowering the opening height.

- In cases in which the mark has proven to be too stringent (and less than the desired number qualify to finals) all the jumpers clearing the next lower height may also be included in the final to bring the number of competitors to the desired level. More than the desired number may qualify as ties are included in this method.

- In the final round, the bar should be started no lower than 4″ (10cm) below the qualifying standard and raised by 2″ (5cm) increments each round until the bar is 2″ (5cm) above the qualifying height or until there are approximately six (6) competitors remaining in the field. At this point, the bar will be raised in 1″ (3cm) increments. When a single competitor remains in the competition, the bar may be placed at the height desired by the competitor.

- In a competition in which there is no qualifying round (as in a one day meet) the starting height of the bar shall be set at the height 2″ (5cm) below that of the mark listed by the lowest ranked competitor as rounded off to the nearest inch. The bar shall then be raised by 2″ (5cm) increments until the height listed by the 6th place jumper is attained. At this point, the bar will be raised by 1″ (3cm) increments.

- When qualifying standards are required such as at state, regional, or national meets, the jumpers should be permitted to begin jumping at a bar height that is lower than the qualifying standard in all fairness to the competitors.

- For combined competition the starting height will be determined by the competitors and will be raised in 1″ (3 cm) increments throughout the competition.

NATIONAL ASSOCIATION FOR GIRLS & WOMEN IN SPORT

8. shall foresee all the needs of contestants, officials, and spectators and ensure that all the technical details of the meet have been taken care of. (Refer to checklist on Meet Organization).

9. shall conduct the coaches meeting at which time scratches, but not additions, will be accepted.

10. may determine that in one day meets, events 400m or longer will be run as finals in sections.

11. shall bar any competitor from remaining events, and invalidate any points scored by her in previous events, if she scratches an event after the coaches meeting without medical verification.

12. shall keep the meet running smoothly and on time.

13. shall approve any times, distances or heights which establish meet records.

14. shall obtain the completed results and records of the meet at its completion and send the official results to all competing teams.

IV. Checklist for Meet Organization

1. Pre-Meet Information

_____ Clear facilities/date/time.

_____ Invite teams, indicating any entry fee.

_____ Secure officials for the meet.

_____ Specify contracted time/date/fee for officials.

_____ Have fees payable at the meet.

_____ Secure stopwatches.

_____ Obtain starting gun, ammunition, red sleeve, whistle.

_____ Obtain scoresheets, pencils, and necessary cards.

_____ Obtain meet hurdles, shotput, discus, javelin and batons.

_____ Obtain Standards and 2-3 bars.

_____ Reserve P.A. system.

_____ Make arrangements for available medical services.

_____ Have available a scale and marker.

_____ Send out time schedule for meet.

_____ Order awards for the meet.

_____ Call press for publicity.

_____ Create a program (if desired).

_____ Seed runners in heats (according to time if possible).

_____ Buy and assign numbers/attach pins.

_____ Secure rooms for officials' meetings and coaches' meeting and lounge.

_____ Secure locker room facilities, towel and lock arrangements.
_____ Obtain video tape equipment, in absence of electronic timing, to assist judges at finish line.

2. Meet Conduct

_____ Be certain the meet begins on time and flows smoothly.
_____ Remember *your* team.
_____ Have confidence in the quality and ability of your lead officials.
_____ Assign "specific" assistance (team guides, press guides, programs handed out, etc.).
_____ You run the coaches' meeting. Be prepared.
_____ Have track markings and rulebook available.

3. Post-Meet Responsibilities

_____ Thank coaches and officials verbally.
_____ Pay officials for their services.
_____ Award trophies/ribbons (may also be done throughout the meet).
_____ Keep all records and file.
_____ Call in results to appropriate media.
_____ Send copies of meet results to coaches or magazines wishing to publish results.
_____ Record meet conditions and publish your own team's results.
_____ Make a final meet report for your files. Include: time, date, place, weather, teams, officials, results and records.

V. Assisting Personnel: Procedures and Techniques

1. Announcer:
a. shall give proper announcements to aid the competitors in reporting to the clerk of course or the field events judges on time. (It is recommended that the first call be given 15 minutes before the event and the final call 5 minutes before the event.)
b. shall inform all competitors of each event and notify finalists to report to their respective events.
c. shall inform the public of the progress of the meet, competitors' names and results of each race or event.
d. should take care not to interfere with the fair running of the meet.
   1. should take care that the announcements do not disturb field events in progress or interrupt the start of the race.

2. should take care that the commentary of a race in progress does not influence the outcome.

2. Scorekeeper:
a. shall have charge of all completed timers' and judges' finish cards and transcribe the results onto a master sheet.
b. shall notify the track referee of the competitors eligible for the semifinals and finals.
c. shall award points for places won to teams that are entered, in order that the team trophy may be awarded.
d. shall see that the announcer gets results of each heat and flights as well as all newly tied or broken records.
e. shall have all records and results checked, approved and signed by the referees.
f. shall turn over all completed records to the meet director at the completion of competition.
g. shall abide by the following scoring procedures:
   1. Points given for the various places are awarded to the competitors' teams and totaled at the conclusion of the meet.
   2. If there is a tie between two or more competitors for any place which receives a score in either a track or field event, the sum of the points of the places involved shall be divided equally between the tying competitors.
   3. If the best performance of a competitor in a field event determined by distance (except high jump) is identical to that of another competitor, the next best effort shall break the tie.
h. shall follow the scoring method described in Rule 2.

3. Wind Gauge (Anemometer) Operator:
a. shall ensure the proper placement of the instrument where required.
b. shall read and record the wind velocity for each long jump, 100 meter hurdle race, and 100 and 200 meter dashes, and report the readings to the scorer where they will be recorded on the event sheet of all preliminaries, trials, qualifying, and final rounds.
c. In the long jump an anemometer shall be placed no more than 20 meters (65'7½") from the take-off board facing the jumper and no farther than 2 meters (6'7") from the runway at a height of 1.22 meters or 4' above the ground. The wind shall be measured for a period of 5 seconds when the competitor starts her approach.

4. Lap Counter:

a. shall count laps and report number of laps remaining to runners as they pass (by means of a large numbered card).

b. any race 3000 meters or more will need a lap counter.

5. Inspector of Implements:

a. shall weigh and measure every implement, including batons, used in competition, and place an identifying mark on each that is approved, prior to the competition.

b. shall impound any implements not meeting competition standards until completion of the competition.

6. Medical Examiner:

a. shall be present prior to the meet to confirm recommendations of the training staff.

b. shall be present at all times during the meet.

c. shall have the authority to allow or deny continued participation by an athlete.

d. shall rule on the necessity of a wrap in any throwing event.

e. shall have access to emergency vehicles at the track.

7. Surveyor:

a. shall inspect and measure the track and all courses and takeoffs for the jumps, throwing circles, scratch lines, landing pits, exchange zones and hurdle spacings. (See Rule 5, Sec. 5 and Rule 6, Sec. 7 and 8 for hurdle, shot put and discus specifications.)

b. shall present a written statement of the findings to the meet director and games committee prior to competition.

8. Marshall:

a. shall keep all areas of the track and field clear and unobstructed as best meets the needs of contestants, officials and spectators.

b. shall make that all unauthorized persons are kept out of the competition areas.

c. shall see that the track is kept clean at all times, and that spectators do not interfere with judges, timers or any official.

d. shall ensure that any infractions which are persistent and unmanageable are reported to the referees and games committee for decision. This could lead to disqualification of competitors and/or teams.

9. Recorder:

a. shall have charge of applications for new records. If any records are broken, shall have the responsibility for seeing that the applications are duly filled out, certified and sent to the proper authorities.

10. **Referee(s):**
   a. in many meets there will be only one referee. In these cases, this referee shall assume the responsibilities of the track referee *and* the field referee. This referee would be titled "meet referee" and would be responsible for the enforcement of all rules and decisions.
   b. shall enforce all rules and decisions and (in the absence of a games committee) decide on all questions not otherwise assigned by the rules.

VI. Track Officials: Procedures and Techniques

1. **Track Referee:**
   a. shall obtain a list of all competitors from the meet director and prior to the start of the meet, place competitors in heats.
      1. shall determine the number of heats by the number of competitors entered and the number of lanes available. (Note Table on following pages)
      2. when past performances are known, determine the fastest competitors and place them in different heats. Example: 6 heats, 6 fastest competitors, one in each heat. 7th fastest competitor is placed in heat #6; 8th fastest in heat #5; 9th fastest in heat #4; 10th fastest in heat #3; 11th fastest in heat #2; 12th fastest in heat #1. The 13th fastest is then placed in heat #1; continue placing the contestants by times working heat #2–#6 and then #6–#1. Try not to place teammates in the same heat.
      3. when times are not known, shall place contestants in any heat, trying not to place teammates in the same heat.
   b. in preliminary heats when three (3) or more competitors are advanced to the succeeding round, quarter finals are required if the number of competitors are more than the maximum number of entries for each of the track tables (6 lanes, 7, 8, & 9). Note tables that follow.
   c. shall supervise the drawing of each lane prior to each trial event for every race and determine placement of competitors in lanes for semifinals and finals by chance drawing of lots for every race. (See Tables.)
   d. shall have charge of all running events and the responsibility for the proper carrying out of the track program.

e.   shall inspect the markings of the track.

f.   shall confer with the chief judges, clerk of course, scorer and starter prior to the meet to be sure that each has sufficient personnel.

g.   shall inform the head officials of the number of heats and the number of competitors who will qualify for the semifinals and finals.

h.   shall ensure that only authorized persons are allowed in the immediate area of the field or arena in cooperation with the marshal.

i.   shall see that all rules are observed and decide any technical points which arise during the meet. In the case where there are not set rules covering a dispute and in the absence of a game committee, the track referee, in coordination with the meet director, shall have the final judgment.

j.   shall have power, if in any race a competitor is disqualified for interfering with another competitor, to order the race to be rerun excluding the disqualified competitor.

k.   shall have the power to exclude any competitor or official for improper conduct or apparel, and decide immediately any protest or objection concerning the conduct of a competitor or official.

l.   shall inspect, approve, and sign the scorer's records upon completion of the competition.

m.   shall have a list of appropriate meet records in all events. American and world records shall be available at all National Championships.

Determination of Heats

Note: The following table can be used in forming heats for dashes, relays, and hurdles:

FOR SIX LANES

No. of Entries	No. of Trial Heats	No. Qualifying	No. of Semifinal Heats	No. Qualifying	No. in Final
1-6	0	—	0	—	6
7-12	0	0	2	3	6
13-18	3	4	2	3	6
19-24	4	3	2	3	6

FOR SEVEN LANES

1-7	0	—	0	—	7
8-14	0	0	2	3+next best time	7
15-21	3	4+2 next best times	2	3+next best time	7
22-28	4	3+2 next best times	2	3+next best time	7

FOR EIGHT LANES

1-8	0	—	0	—	1-8
9-16	0	0	2	3+next 2 best times	8
17-24	3	4+next 4 best times	2	4	8
25-32	4	3 + next 4 best times	2	4	8
33-40	5	2+next 6 best times	2	4	8

FOR NINE LANES

1-9	0	—	0	—	1-9
10-18	0	0	2	4+next best time	9
19-27	0	0	3	2+next 3 best times	9
28-36	4	6+3 next 3 best times	3	3	9
37-45	5	5+next 2 best times	3	3	9
46-54	6	4+next 3 best times	3	3	9
55-63	7	4+next best time	3	3	9
64-72	8	3+next 3 best times	3	3	9
73-81	9	3	3	3	9

WHERE FULLY AUTOMATIC TIMING IS USED
FOR EIGHT LANES

1-8	0	—	0	—	1-8
9-16	0	0	2	3+next 2 best times	8
17-24	3	4+next 4 best times	2	4	8
25-32	4	3+next 4 best times	2	4	8
33-40	5	2+next 6 best times	2	4	8

FOR NINE LANES

1-9	0	—	0	—	1-9
10-18	0	0	2	4+next best time	9
19-27	0	0	3	2+next 3 best times	9
28-36	4	6+3 next 3 best times	3	3	9
37-45	5	5+next 2 best times	3	3	9
46-54	6	4+next 3 best times	3	3	9
55-63	7	4+next best times	3	3	9
64-72	8	3+next 3 best times	3	3	9
73-81	9	3	3	3	9

Forming of Heats after the First Round of the Competition:
1. Give first consideration to the place that the competitors finished in the previous round.
2. Time is considered *after* place in the forming of heats.
3. Working from left to right and right to left:
   a. Group and seed first place winners by their times.
   b. Group and seed second place winners by their times.
   c. Continue for as many places qualified.

CODE (or KEY)

    1a = Fastest first place winner
    1b = Second fastest first place winner
    1c = Third fastest first place winner
    2a = Fastest second place winner
    2b = Second fastest second place winner

d.   If two contestants from the same team fall within the same heat, move the slower runner to another heat by interchanging with a runner of nearest comparable place and time (weighing place first and time second).

2. Clerk of Course:

a.   shall obtain from the track referee the name and number of all competitors in their respective events and heats.

b.   shall have the announcer notify competitors to appear at the designated area before the start of each event in which they are entered.

c.   shall report to the track referee, the name(s) of any competitor who does not report at least 15 minutes (or within the time established by the meet director) before her event is scheduled.

d.   shall ensure that the competitors are in their assigned lanes and are utilizing the proper starting line for a particular event; and that the timers and finish judges are stationed at the proper finish line.

TABLES:

Table 1. 3 heats formed from preceeding rounds of four heats, qualifying on a nine (9) lane track.

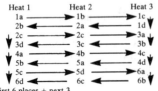

first 6 places + next 3 best times (a, b, c)

Table 3. 2 heats formed from preceding rounds of four (4) heats, qualifying on an eight (8) lane track.

first 4 places

Table 2. 2 heats formed from preceding rounds of three heats, qualifying on an eight (8) lane track.

first 5 places + next best time (a)

Table 4. 2 heats formed from preceding rounds of five (5) heats, qualifying on an eight (8) lane track.

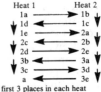

first 3 places in each heat + next best time (a)

Table 5. 2 heats formed from preceding rounds of four (4) heats, qualifying on a six (6) lane track.

Heat 1	Heat 2
1a	1b
1d	1c
2b	2a
2c	2d
3a	3b
3d	3c

Table 6. 2 heats formed from preceding rounds of three heats qualifying on a six (6) lane track.

Heat 1	Heat 2
1a	1b
2a	1c
2b	2c
3b	3a
3c	4a
4c	4b

e. shall ensure that starting blocks (when used) are placed at the proper starting line.

f. shall have competitors lined up several heats in advance if there are a number of heats to be run in any event.

g. shall give instructions to all heats of an event at the same time, prior to the first heat relative to: the starting procedures, length of the event, the number of qualifiers, the finish line, false starts, cutting in, lap time, remaining in their lanes, etc.

h. shall check the runners' spikes to ensure they are in correspondence with the rules of the track.

i. shall verify that all batons have been officially approved.

j. shall ensure that the members of each starting team in relay races have been properly selected:
   1. shall preregister prior to the meet and the clerk shall check their card; or
   2. shall register at the line at the time of the competition; or
   3. shall draw for a lane upon arrival.

k. In all cases the clerk of course shall circle the anchor number and place it on the heat sheet.

l. shall provide the chief finish judge with a card with the names of the competitors, their numbers, and their assigned lanes.

m. shall work in conjunction with the starter at all times.

3. Starter and Assistant Starter:

a. shall wear a colored sleeve on the gun arm that will be clearly discernible to the judges and timers.

b. shall give these commands in races of 400 meters (440 yards) or less—"On your mark," (after competitors are in their blocks and become motionless—approximately 12-15 seconds—the starter shall give the command "Set") "Set," (wait until all competitors are motionless—approximately two seconds) and fire the gun or give another signal.

c. in races over 400 meters (440 yards), the starting commands shall be "Runners Set" and when all the competitors are ready, the gun shall be fired. This time does not usually exceed two seconds.

d. if the competitors on the mark are nervous or unsteady, have them stand up and attempt to steady their nerves. This must be done before the gun fires or it is a false start.

e. may use whistle commands rather than vocal when using staggered starts to ensure being heard. A long, loud blast should be used for each voice command, then the gun fires. Competitors should be so instructed.

f. shall make sure that each competitor is on the proper mark and that any part of the body that is in contact with the ground is behind the starting line. (The baton may touch the ground in front of the starting line.)

g. when blocks are used (440 and less), both hands and feet must be in contact with the ground.

h. shall warn or disqualify any competitor who is disconcerting to other competitors.

i. shall be the sole judge of anyone making a false start and, if the gun has already been fired, recall the competitors by again firing the gun. If a competitor makes a false start before the gun has been fired, the starter shall call everybody off their marks, and the clerk of course shall reassemble the competitors.

j. may recall competitors following an unfair start which is not the fault of any of the competitors, without assessing any penalty.

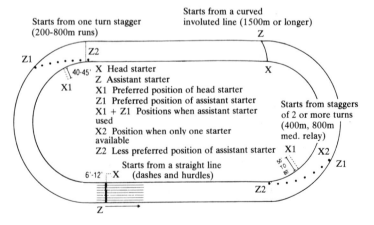

Figure 15. Starts.

k. shall recall competitors if a runner is jostled and falls, or is placed at a distinct disadvantage, while in the first turn of a race not run in lanes, or as the runners move into the straightaway after running one turn in lanes, as in the 800m run.

l. shall warn the competitor by saying, "You have one false start; one more, and you will be disqualified." (3 false starts are allowed in the combined events.)

m. shall stand in such a position that all the competitors are clearly visible and that the sound of the gun should carry as equal a distance as possible to all competitors. The head starter's gun must be clearly visible to the times. (See Figure 15.)

Starting positions for the starter (and assistant starter when available) for the following types of races:

1. Races on the straightaway (short dashes and hurdles)—
   a. When a single starter is used: The starter must stand in a position so that the entire field of competitors may be viewed, and so that the starting gun as held by the starter is clearly visible to the judges. The best position to view the runners at their marks is approximately 6 to 12 feet in front of the starting line and from 6 to 12 feet away from the nearest lane. Since the stands are usually located within a few feet of the outside lane, most starters prefer to position themselves on the infield on the inside of the track in order to obtain a more advantageous position for viewing the start. From this position all the lanes may be viewed without moving the eyes.
   b. When an assistant starter is used: the assistant starter stands on the opposite side of the track and looks down the starting line.

2. Races with a one-turn stagger (200 meter dash and 800 meter run)—
   a. When a single starter is used: the starter must stand in a position so that the entire field may be viewed in a single glance without shifting the focus of the eyes. Either of two (2) positions may be taken. In the first position, the starter is positioned 40-50 ft. inside the inner lane of the track and even with the middle runner of the field. The distance from the innermost competitor to the outermost competitor lane may vary from 50 to 80 feet depending on the number and the width of the lanes.

   Obviously the starter may have to move farther away from the track in order to view all competitors simultaneously. This method places the gun approximately equidistant from all competitors enabling them to obtain an equal start. This position is also used by the head starter when an assistant starter is available.

The second method positions the starter on the track at approximately the middle lane and slightly in front of the competitor in the outside lane. From this position, the starter is able to look more down the line of the competitors while catching any movement in the outside lane with peripheral vision. The disadvantages of this start are that the starter must immediately move off the track in order not to interfere with the competitors in the inside lanes and the competitors in the outside lanes will hear the sound of the gun slightly ahead of the competitors in the inner lanes. However, this advantage for the outside lane is practically negligible in the one-turn stagger since the competitors are in closer proximity than in the longer staggers.

b. When an assistant starter is used: the assistant starter stands outside the outer lane of the track in advance of the competitor in the outside lane in such a position that the entire line of competitors may be viewed.

In the 800 meter run, the assistant starter will watch closely for any jostling, impeding of progress, or unavoidable contact as the competitors run in lanes around the curve to the breakpoint. The assistant starter should move behind the competitors on the outside of the track to obtain a different view of the race from that of the starter, and will also fire a recall shot if a competitor is fouled or unfairly impeded.

3. Races with a two- or more turn stagger (400 meter run and 400 meter relay, 800 meter relay, 800 meter medley relay, mile relay)—

a. When a single starter is used: the only position a single starter may take in a field where competitors may be staggered from the inside to the outside lanes (from 100 to 160 feet) depending on the number and width of lanes, is at the middle of the track slightly in advance of the outside competitor. This position permits the starter to look down the line of competitors in a single focus catching any movement in the outside lane with peripheral vision. The disadvantage of this start is that the gun is a considerable distance from the competitor(s) in the inside lane(s). Competitors in the outside lanes would have an advantage from hearing the gun earlier. Races of this type require the use of an assistant for the fair and most effective starting procedures. In this situation, the head starter then occupies a position on the infield opposite the competitor in the middle lane; and at such a distance from the competitors that half the field may be observed without shifting the focus. When the competitors are called to the set position, the starter's eyes shall sweep down the line of competitors observing their readiness and then focus on the half of the field that is the head starter's responsibility before the firing of the gun. When the assistant starter is positioned in advance of the outside competitor, the head starter is usually responsible for the competitors on the inside half of the track. However, if the assistant is positioned on the inside lane behind the first competitor, then the responsibility of the head starter is with the competitors in the outside lanes.

b. When an assistant starter is used: the assistant starter may take one of two positions. The preferred position places the assistant starter outside the track in advance of the competitor in the outer lane in such a way that the assistant starter may look down the line of competitors. When the head starter—from a position on the infield—takes the responsibility of the competitors on the inside of the track, the assistant starter then takes principal responsibility for the competitors on the outside of the track. However, the assistant starter should fire a recall shot when any competitor is observed making an illegal start.

The second position places the assistant starter to the rear of the competitors on the inside lane in such a way that the entire line of competitors is visible. The principal responsibility of the assistant starter is the competitors in the inner lanes. In this case, the head starter is responsible for the competitors in the outer lanes.

4. Races from a curved involuted (waterfall) start (1500 meters, mile, or longer).

a. When a single starter is used: the starter stands in advance of the competitors on the inside of the track at a distance that the entire field is visible. After firing the gun, the starter follows the competitors as they move to the inside lanes and obtain racing positions. Any fouling or entanglements—whether intentional or unavoidable—would create a situation in which the race could be recalled. This could occur within the first 100 to 150 yards of the race.

b. When an assistant starter is used: the assistant starter is preferably placed to the outside of the track and in advance of the outermost competitor so that a good view of the starting line is available. Also, this puts the assistant starter in a position to follow the progress of the competitors during the first crucial yards as they maneuver for a racing position.

c. *Note:* In the 1500 meter run which begins on the straightaway and in the other races which begin on a curve, both starters must move with the field after the firing of the gun. The head starter, from a position on the infield, may move across the field to the straightaway in races started on the curve. The assistant starter would move on to the track and follow the race from the rear.

Note: When competitors are positioned in a staggered start, the head starter may find it advantageous to stand on a low platform or box two (2) or three (3) feet in height in order that a clear view may be obtained. When the assistant starter is standing outside the track in advance of the outermost competitor, a box may also be of advantage, particularly in races in which a two-turn stagger or more is used. (For instance, in the 800 meter relay—4×200m—as run entirely in lanes, the distance from the competitor in the first lane to the competitor in the eighth lane on a track with 42″ wide lanes would be over 300 feet. Obviously the starters need every advantage in obtaining the clearest view of the field.)

Note: When the head starter is using a gun which is connected to an electric timing device, a second gun shall be available for recalling the start in order that the gun connected to the electric timing device may be laid down and not hinder the starter as the starter moves across the infield following the competitors.

n. shall inform the competitors unless the clerk has already done so where and when they may cut to the inside lane in relays and races where only a portion of the event is run in lanes.

o.   shall use a starting gun of not less than .32 caliber with powder giving a distinct flash, and hold the gun in such a manner as to provide a background against which the flash is clearly discernible. When a gun is non-functioning or unavailable a short, quick blast of a whistle can be used for the start signal.

p.   shall always have at least two shells in the gun before starting any race. Live ammunition is never used.

q.   shall rule on all questions concerning the start and have entire control of the competitors on their marks.

r.   shall decide in conjunction with the clerk which one will have instructional responsibilities to the competitors.

s.   shall have a recall starter whenever possible to assist with the start of each race.

t.   shall use hand signals to indicate to the timers what the runners are doing.
1. The starter shall blow a whistle to indicate runners are ready. Upon hearing a responsive whistle from the chief timekeeper, the starter shall proceed.
2. "On your marks"—the starter shall raise the gun hand over the head in a position clearly visible to the timers.
3. "Set"—free hand is raised.
4. The gun is fired when all runners are motionless. (Reaction times indicate that a minimum of 1.4 sec. are needed for optimum starts. International starters may hold runners several seconds.)

4. Chief Finish Judge:
a.   shall assign finish places to all judges. At least 2 judges should be assigned to each place to be picked and shall be instructed to serve at opposite sides of the track.

b.   shall see that the finish string is ready and that someone has been appointed to hold it if there are no posts available.

c.   shall have 1 or 2 assistants to help with the duties and carry messages such as the finish cards to the scorer.

d.   shall make arrangements to place the judges of the finish on elevated stands at a recommended distance of 6' from the edge of the track and directly across from the finish line.

e.   shall instruct the judges to watch the race until the competitors are within 10 meters of the finish line, and then concentrate on the space above the finish line.

f.   shall instruct the judges that they are to make their own decisions without discussion or comparison with other judges and timers.

g. shall check to see that all judges are ready when the starter blows the whistle and reports to the chief timekeeper that all judges are ready.

h. shall note the finish of each competitor in order to issue a decision in case of a disagreement between judges. In the event that a competitor should be overlooked by all the judges, i.e., if the competitor did finish in a placing position but was not picked by the place judges, the chief judge may place the competitor so overlooked in the position in which the chief judge *saw* the competitor finish. If in the absence of a photo-print, or video tape replay moved through the recorder by hand, the chief judge cannot come to a decision after conferring with the track referee, then the original placings shall stand.

i. shall write on the heat card received from the clerk of course the places of the competitors as indicated by the judges at the conclusion of each race. If necessary, indicate that the competitor did not finish or was disqualified. The card should be signed and given to the chief timekeeper.

j. a sample of a "Chief Finish Judge and Chief Timer's Report" card follows. A 5" × 8" card should be used. *Final* heat cards should be of a different color from the other heats.

5. Finish Judge(s):

a. shall stand at the side of the track directly opposite the finish line, preferably on an elevated platform, in order to have an unobstructed view of the finish line whenever possible.

b. shall pick the competitor at the moment any part of the torso, (i.e., torso-as distinguished from the head, neck, arms, legs, or feet) crosses the perpendicular plane of the nearest edge of the finish line.

c. as the competitors approach the finish, the judge shall cease to follow the competitor and focus the eyes on the space above the finish line. For example, if picking third place, the judge may count mentally while focusing on the finish line, and looking straight across and count "one, two, three" as the competitors cross the finish line.

d. shall immediately notify the chief finish judge of the decision at the finish of each race.

e. shall not discuss with other judges the outcome of the race until after the chief judge has been notified.

CHIEF FINISH JUDGE AND CHIEF TIMER'S REPORT

Meet _____ Date _____ Event _____ Heat _____
Chief Finish Judge _____ Chief Timekeeper _____
Lane ____ No. ____ Competitor ____ School/Org. ___ Time ____ Place ____

Lane						
1						
2						
3						
4						
5						
6						
7						
8						
9						

6. Chief Timekeeper:

a. shall obtain a list of meet, American and world records.

b. shall have one or two assistant runners to and from the clerk and the scorers table.

c. shall be sure all watches are numbered and that the name of the person using each watch is recorded along with the number.

d. shall see that watches are synchronized before being assigned to timekeepers. Test them by touching the stems of two watches together to start and stop them, to see if they are running in time with each other. All watches should be checked in this manner. The watches that run closest together should be assigned first and second places.

e. shall assign place finishes to all timekeepers.

f. shall check to see that all timekeepers and finish judges are ready when the starter blows the whistle and signal back to the starter that all are ready. Then, the chief timekeeper shall call out "Gun is up."

g. ___ctr___ ic timing equ___ ___ ___ ht ___ ___ ___ be used when avai ___ le. H___ ___-___r, ___ rangements ___ ___ ___ an___ ___ ning must be ma___ ___o as___ ___re ___ ___icia ___ imes in the e___ ___ he___ le ___onic timing devic___ ___ils ___ ___ ly ___om ___ic timing is a ___ ___ le tri___ ___ti___ ng device v/hich is ___rte ___ ___ a ___ ___tac___ on the start___ ___ ___ ist ___ ___ any similar appa___ ___s at ___ ___e ___ ___tan ___ f the flash ___ ___n th___ ___ ___rge. The finishin___ ___imes ___ ___n ___ ___ren ___ nts of 1/100t___ ___ e___ ___n___ a ___ l the finish places ___ ___he c___ ___-___ ___ito___ shall be reac ___ o ___ a ___h ___o-finish (m___oving) ___tu___re

h. shall be in such a position as to time first place and more places if possible. In a case where the watches fail to catch a time for a place, no time shall be recorded for that place.

i. shall check each watch as the time is given by the timekeeper, record the times of the contestants in 1/10 of sec. When converting a time from 1/100 to 1/10 of a sec., round it to the next longer 1/10 of a sec. (e.g., 55.44 becomes 55.5). Hand the card to a runner who will take it to the scorer.

j. shall rule on the official time as follows:
   1. if there are three watches on one place and all three watches show different times, the middle time is official (not the average of the three).
   2. if two of the three watches are the same and one is different, the time in which two are identical is official.
   3. if there are only two watches on a place with each showing a different time, the slower of the two is considered official time.
   4. if there is a record performance, the chief timekeeper shall read, record, and document all 3 watches.

k. In the case of a second place time being faster than the first place time, consider the second place time to be wrong, and record it as "no time." The chief timekeeper with the track referee when a time of "no-time" is recorded.

l. shall order all watches cleared and made ready for the next race after all times have been duly inspected and recorded.

m. *Note:* In the pentathlon events, the chief timekeeper shall assign, read and record 3 watches on each competitor in each event.

7. Timekeepers:

a. shall be positioned at the finish line in such a manner as to look directly across the line.

b. shall check the watch before the start of the meet with the chief timekeeper and become familiar with the type of watch.

c. shall check periodically to make certain the watch is properly wound during the progress of the meet.

d. shall start the watch from the flash or the smoke of the pistol and stop it at the moment that any part of the torso (i.e., torso, as distinguished from head, neck, arms, legs, or feet) crosses the perpendicular plane of the nearest edge of the finish line. As the competitors approach the finish, the timekeeper shall cease to follow the competition and shall focus the eyes on the space just above the finish line.

e. shall have no discussion with the other timekeepers about the times of the runner in the event.

f. shall use good timing techniques:
   1. hold the watch lightly in the hand with the index finger on the stem. The index finger must be given full freedom to move.
   2. practice starting and stopping the watch until you get the feel of the action of the stem. When preparing to time, take up the slack (extra movement) in the stem by pressing it until the slightest extra movement will start the watch.
   3. squeeze the stem slowly, as you would the trigger of a gun; only the index finger moves.
   4. the time is taken from the flash of the pistol to the moment that any part of the torso of the competitor reaches the nearest edge of the finish line.
   5. if the hand of the watch stops between the two lines indicating the time, the nearest slowest tenth shall be accepted (i.e., 12.1+ shall be 12.2).
   6. Timepieces must be calibrated so that at least one-tenth of a second is measurable. Electronic timers which measure one hundredth of a second are preferred.

g. shall record the time of the watch on timer's slip and give it to the chief timekeeper; or give the time verbally if the chief timekeeper requests.

h. shall inform the chief timekeeper of any malfunction in the watch immediately.

i. shall wait until the chief timekeeper gives instructions before clearing the watch.

j. shall return the watch to the chief timekeeper and check off name at the end of the running events.

8. Inspectors:

a. shall be at least 6 in number, one of whom is designated as the chief inspector.

b. shall have no right or authority to make decisions but must report all infractions or irregularities of the rules to the chief inspector immediately after the race. (The chief inspector will report directly to the track referee. When all facts concerning the infraction have been reviewed, the referee decides if there has been a violation of the rules.)

c. Two inspectors shall stand behind the starting line in hurdle race and dashes. The others are stationed at intervals along the track.

d. In races where each competitor runs in a lane and must round a curve, it is the duty of the inspector, stationed on the curve, to see that each competitor stays in the appropriate lane and makes no foul.

e. For races in lanes around turns, an inspector should be assigned 2 lanes for the entire turn with the responsibility for seeing whether or not the runners remain in their respective lanes.

f. shall place themselves so as to cover each passing zone and shall be certain that the baton is passed within the passing zone in relay races.

g. shall watch to see that a competitor who has finished the baton pass does not interfere with the baton passing of the competitors on opposing teams. (Refer to rules governing relay racing.)

h. shall have 2 flags to designate the readiness of competitors and/or rule infractions which might occur.

i. The chief of inspectors shall be responsible for the proper placement, height, and weight of the hurdles.

j. In shuttle relays, watch to see that:
   1. the incoming runner taps the next runner on the right shoulder
      or
   2. in the alternate method, that some part of the incoming runner's torso breaks the plane of the restraining line, 4' in front of the starting line, before the next runner starts.

9. **Race Walk Inspectors**
   a. There shall be a minimum of four inspectors and one chief inspector (track referee).
   b. The chief inspector shall:
      1. meet with the inspectors prior to the start of the race, brief them on their duties, assign each to supervise a specific portion of the track, and provide them with pencils and cards with which to record cautions.
      2. be in a position to oversee the entire race and not be confined to a given section of the track.
      3. move into a position from which to more closely observe a competitor when a caution has been received from an inspector.
      4. warn the competitor of the caution and the reason for it.
      5. disqualify a competitor for:
         a) 2 cautions, if one is given by the chief inspector at a point different from the other inspector

b) 3 cautions, from three inspectors for infractions occurring at different points in the race

c) a single infraction if violation of form is flagrant

6. inform the competitor by waving a white flag for a caution or a red flag for a disqualification in front of the competitor.

7. direct any disqualified competitor to leave the track.

8. at the end of the race, collect the remaining cards from the inspectors, note any further disqualifications and make a final report to the head finish judge.

c. The inspectors shall:

1. stand or kneel on the outside lanes of the track and view the walkers coming toward them. If there is any question of possible infraction, continue walking backward with the competitor while making decision.

2. record a caution on the card if the walker violates the rules by noting:

a) competitors number

b) point of infraction (time, place on track)

c) type of infraction with the following symbols:
   —lifting (doubtful contact)
   —creeping (bent support leg)

3. be aware of three areas where walkers may be particularly susceptible to infractions; the start and finish, and when passing another competitor.

4. deliver card to chief inspector as soon as caution is noted. Note at the bottom if you feel the infraction is flagrant.

VII. Field Officials: Procedures and Techniques

1. Field Referee:

a. shall be in charge of all field events and be responsible for the proper carrying out of the field event program.

b. shall inspect all throwing areas to determine if sectors and scratch lines are clearly marked.

c. shall inspect jumping pits, runways, and cross bars for the jumping events.

d. shall make certain that equipment for all field events is available.

e. shall take the place of the inspector of implements, assuming those responsibilities in smaller meets.

f. shall rule on the use of a competitor's personal equipment (shot put, discus, or javelin). Any such implement which is ruled official may be used by any competitor if so desired.

g. shall make certain there are sufficient judges and assistants for all field events.

h. shall make sure all field judges and assistants know and understand their duties, methods of measuring, and what constitutes a foul in that event and shall maintain constant supervision throughout the competition.

i. shall obtain the list of competitors for field events from the meet director and determine the order of competition and number of finalists before the day of the meet. This order of competition in each event shall be turned over to the head field judge in charge of each event.

j. shall see that field events start on time.

k. shall rule on all questions pertaining to field events.

l. shall be responsible for conducting competition in the throwing events and the long jump using any of the following procedures:

- Competitors each have one trial in first round, one in second, etc.
- Competitors may have two successive trials in first round and one in second round.
- Competitors may be divided into flights which shall be determined as follows:

  1. Competitors shall be assigned to preliminary round flights by lot in a left to right, right to left alternating sequence. Example:

Order	Flight 1	Flight 2	Flight 3
1	A	B	C
2	F	E	D
3	G	H	I
4	L	K	J

     This process will also determine the order of competition in each flight.

  2. If two competitors from the same team are in the same flight, one may be exchanged with a competitor in the same order from an adjacent flight. Should this still place two competitors from a team in the same flight, make the exchange from the nearest possible flight without a competitor from that team. (In the above example, if A, F and K were from the same team, A could exchange with C, or F could exchange with D.)

  3. All competitors in one flight shall complete all preliminary trials before the next flight begins preliminary round trials.

4. When the number of competitors exceeds ten, it is rec-ommended that two flights be used. Additional flights may be required to keep the number of competitors in each flight to not less than six nor more than ten.

m. shall see that the number of finalists in field events corresponds with the maximum number of finalists to be selected in track events run in lanes. The order of competition in the final round shall be determined by lot.

n. In the high jump competition, if there are enough competitors to warrant it, flights of no more than 6 to 8 may be used. An entire flight will clear or miss the height before the next flight begins its attempts. When the number of jumpers competing becomes smaller, the flights may be combined. Note: revolving method on page 179.

o. shall sign each event sheet following trials and finals.

p. When, during the warmup period, the opening height proves to be too stringent for *all* competitors this should be reported to the meet director who should take appropriate action by lowering the opening height.

2. Head Field Judge of Each Field Event

a. shall see that competitors report at least 15 minutes (or within the time established by the meet director) before the event is scheduled. Report to the field referee the name(s) of any competitor who does not check in on time.

b. shall supervise the competitor's drawing if the order of competition has not been decided in advance.

c. shall see that the necessary equipment is available (implements, measuring instruments, markers, rakes, brooms, crossbars, stopwatches, sand or plasticine for the take-off board, etc.). Each judge shall inspect the area for which the judge is responsible—jumping pits and throwing areas.

d. shall instruct field judges and assistants as to their duties, methods of measuring, what constitutes a foul, etc.

e. shall see that all implements have been checked and marked by the inspector of implements or, in her/his absence, by the field referee. Any implements not so checked by the start of competition shall not be used.

f. shall advise competitors as to runways, sectors, and scratch lines, order of competition, number to qualify for finals, etc.

g. shall instruct competitors to be ready to perform as soon as the competitor preceding them has finished the trial. Each competitor is allowed 90 seconds from the time she is called up until the time she initiates her trial.

h. shall make sure competitors who are competing in more than one event understand that they are to report back to the head field judge in that event when they have finished participating in the other event(s) or after each trial, flight or round if it is another field event.

Note: In situations in which a field event competitor is also competing in a running event and there is a schedule conflict, the following procedures are to be followed:

1. If the competitor must report to the running event during the conduct of her field event, she shall report to the head field judge who will note on the recording sheet the event to which she is called.

2. The competitor will have a maximum of ten minutes following the completion of her running event to return to her field event and be prepared to initiate warm-up/trial as directed by the head field judge. (The judge may record the time at which the event ended or the meet director may require the competitor to obtain a card from the head timer noting the time her running event ended.)

3. Upon her return, the competitor shall be allowed two warm-up throws or run-throughs if she did not attempt any before being called to the running event. These warm-ups may be taken during the round in progress. The warm-ups should not be consecutive. No additional warm-ups are given if any were taken prior to leaving for the running event.

4. In dual or triangular meets, a competitor in this situation may take a maximum of two consecutive trials to replace the trial(s) missed while running or taking warm-ups.

5. In meets with four or more teams, a competitor may have her two warmup throws or run-throughs. The head judge should try to schedule warm-ups in such a way as to cause the competitor to miss the least number of trials. The competitor may not have more than one trial in a single round of competition. Trials missed in a previous round may not be made up. The competitor may elect to pass her warm-up and have her first attempt count as a trial.

6. In the high jump, the competitor may take her two warmup attempts either:

   a) at the height of the cross bar upon her return, *or*
   b) without the cross bar.

At no time shall the cross bar be lowered once the competition has started.

i.   shall call competitors in the following manner: "Brown, Smith and Jones; Brown up." Then after Brown jumps call: "Smith, Jones, and Simmons; Smith up," etc.

j.   shall read and record measurements for all field events immediately after each throw or jump.

k.   shall call a foul the instant it occurs by calling out clearly "Foul," and immediately raising the red flag in their possession to indicate a foul. If the jump or throw is good, they shall raise the other flag.

l.   shall watch for fouls by standing in the following positions:
    1. shotput: stand to the open side of the competitor so the full motion of the put might be observed (see Rule 6; sec. 7).
    2. discus and standing long jump: stand to the side of the competitor (see Rule 6; sec. 5 & 8).
    3. running long jump: stand beside the take-off board, focusing eyes on the take-off board (see Rule 6; sec. 4).
    4. javelin and softball throws: stand at the scratch line of the arc (see Rule 6; sec. 9 & 10).
    5. high jump: stand beside the jumping standard in position to observe the plane of the bar to the ground (see Rule 6; sec. 3).

m.   shall declare a foul if an implement lands on a sector line.

n.   shall declare a foul if a competitor fails to leave the runway from behind the scratch line arc and the lines drawn from the extremities of the arc after the throw has been marked in the javelin event.

o.   shall record a throw or jump on which a foul occurs as a trial but will not measure the throw or jump.

p.   shall record distances in discus and javelin throws in even 2 centimeters (1") units to the nearest unit below distance covered. All other distances shall be recorded to the nearest 1 centimeter (¼") below the distance covered.

q.   All measurements must be made with a steel or fiberglass tape graduated in centimeters or quarter inches for the mark to be submitted for a record.

r.   shall stress safety precautions with both the competitors and the assistants.

s.   Head Field Judges: throwing, standing and running long jump events.

    1. Use the following measuring techniques:
       • Measurements of shotput and discus throw: mea-

surements shall be made from nearest mark made by fall of implement to inside edge of circle circumference along a line from mark of implement to center of circle. Zero end of tape should be held at mark of implement. Measurement may be found by moving the tape through an arc along inside edge of circle until the shortest distance is found.

- Measurement of softball and javelin throws (when javelin is thrown from a scratch line) shall be made from nearest mark made by implement to inside edge of scratch line. Zero end of tape shall be held at mark of implement.
- Measurement of javelin and softball throws where scratch line arc is used, shall be taken at the inner edge of the circumference of the arc. Such measurements shall be made on a line from the nearest mark made by the point of the javelin (the tip must strike the ground first) to the center of the circle of which the arc is a part. Zero end of tape shall be at mark of implement.
- Measurement of long jump is made from nearest mark in pit made by any part of the body or limbs to edge of take-off board nearest the pit. Zero end of tape shall be held at break in pit—use a pencil or metal shaft through metal loop of tape to hold secure in the sand while measuring. Tape must be stretched at right angles to take-off board or its extension.

2. shall supervise practice rounds to ensure that only 3 trials are taken.
3. shall designate take-off board to be used for measurement. If the competitor takes off before the board, it is legal but measurement is taken only from the board.
4. shall credit each competitor with the best of all the competitor's preliminary and final trials. If a qualifying round is necessary, performances made during the qualifying round will *not* be used for final placings, but may count as meet or other records.
5. shall signal to assistants to prepare or clear the area, and when the area is in order announce the next competitor.
6. NOTE: THE SOMERSAULT STYLE JUMP IS PROHIBITED.
7. shall determine the finalists in each event and their order of competition drawn by lot for the finals. Once determined they shall be confirmed by the field referee.

8. shall send names of those who qualify for finals to the scorer after referee has approved them. Results should be announced and competitors informed as to who has qualified for finals.
9. shall determine how competitors finished after finals are completed, sign event sheets, and send final results to the field referee.
10. shall, upon receiving the field referee's signature, send the final results to the scorer.
11. shall see that field judges or assistants collect and return equipment to custodian.

t. Head Field Judge: high jump
1. shall announce the starting height and the subsequent heights to which the bar will be raised at the end of each round. (See Rule 6, b.2 for specified increments.)
2. shall approve the type of marks and their placement used by competitors on the apron.
3. shall, if there are enough competitors to warrant it, use flights of no more than 6 to 8. An entire flight will clear or miss the height before the next flight begins its attempts. When the number of jumpers competing becomes smaller, the flights may be combined.

   A REVOLVING FLIGHT SYSTEM of competing may be used and is generally preferred. In this method, the first 3, 4 or 5 competitors may constitute a flight. As a competitor clears the bar, passes a turn at the height, or is eliminated, the next competitor in order will be moved up. This permits the number of competitors active to remain constant and prevents competitors from either having too long a wait or too little rest between jumps at a particular height.
4. Measurement in the high jump shall be made in a perpendicular line from a point on the same level as the take-off to the lowest point on the top side of the crossbar. Measurement of height of crossbar (both the center and the ends of the bar at the standards) shall be made each time the bar is raised to a new height or replaced after a missed trial. To reduce the delay in measuring each time the cross bar is replaced after a miss, it is strongly recommended that a steel or be glass tape, graduated in centimeters or quarter inches, be attached to a stick and used to check the height of the cross bar.

   The center of the bar is the official height and the ends will measure approximately ⅞" higher than the center.

The bar shall be marked so that the same side is always facing up.

5. shall record misses at each height in the high jump.

   Note: Which direction the jumper leaves the pit following a jump or whether or not the bar falls off before the jumper leaves the pit is irrelevant. The bar must remain on the standards immediately following the jump to be a successful jump. If a jumper, when jumping, touches the landing area with her foot, and in the opinion of the official no advantage is gained, the jump should not be considered a failure.

6. shall announce misses in this way in the high jump: "First miss, Second miss, Final miss."

   Note: If a competitor has two misses and passes her last attempt at a height, she must clear the cross bar on her first jump at the next height she attempts in order to remain in the competition.

7. shall wait until the bar is replaced and make sure that the bar is still and not shaking in the wind.

8. shall run the high jump from start to completion for all competitors entered in the event.

9. shall in the event of a tie, implement the following tie breaking order:

   a) the competitor with the lowest number of trials for the height at which the tie occurs shall be awarded the higher place.

   b) if the tie still remains, the competitor with the lowest total number of misses throughout the competition (up to and including the height last cleared) shall be awarded the higher place.

   c) if the tie remains after applying (a) and (b):

      1) If it concerns first place, the competitors tying shall have one more attempt for the height at which they failed and, if no decision is reached, the bar shall be lowered or raised by intervals of 1″ and each competitor shall try at once at each height until the winner is determined. No set height greater than that at which the tie occurred may be registered as the winning height.

      2) If it concerns any place other than first place, the competitors shall be awarded the same place in the competition.

10. No misses should be charged to a competitor for a passed height.

u. Field Judge/Assistants
1. shall report directly to the head field judge at least 15 minutes prior to the event for instructions.
2. shall mark the spot where an implement first touches the ground immediately after the trial in the throwing events and shall not retrieve the implement until the throw has been properly marked.
3. shall see that implements are returned to the throwing area at the proper time.
4. shall measure distances immediately after each trial.
5. shall make all measurements of height and distance with a steel or fiberglass tape graduated in quarter inches and/or centimeters if a record is to be admitted.
6. shall measure both ends of the bar and the center when raising to a new height.
7. shall raise the bar when indicated by the heat field judge in the high jump. Replace the bar with the same side always toward the competitor (side may have an identifying mark on it).
8. shall remeasure the center of the bar after each miss.
9. javelin assistants shall have 2 flags of different colors; red to indicate a foul landing, the other to indicate a fair throw.
10. shall promote safety precautions for spectators, competitors, and other officials by enforcing the following:
    a) the long jump rake is always kept prongs down and away from the pit.
    b) the long jump pit shall be raked between jumps under the direction of the field judge, and not as a competitor approaches.
    c) throwing implements should be handed back to the thrower, and not thrown back in return.
11. shall stand away from the pit so as not to distract competitors.
12. shall collect the equipment at the end of the preliminaries or finals and return it to the custodian of equipment, or other assigned personnel.

CHARTS FOR MEASURING FIELD EVENTS

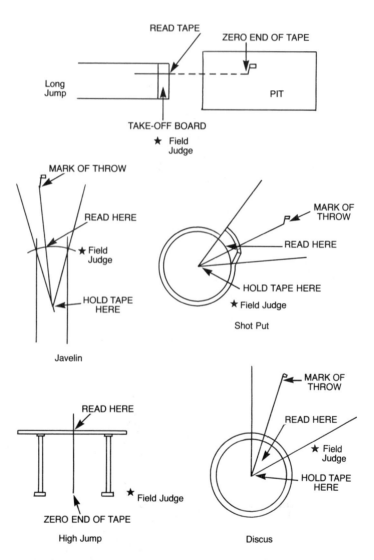

Long Jump

High Jump

Javelin

Shot Put

Discus

DIAGRAMS FOR LAYING OUT THROWING AREAS

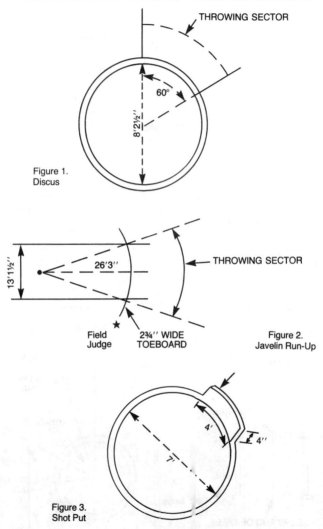

THROWING SECTOR

60°

8'2½"

Figure 1.
Discus

THROWING SECTOR

13'1½"

26'3"

Field
Judge

2¾" WIDE
TOEBOARD

Figure 2.
Javelin Run-Up

4'

4"

7'

Figure 3.
Shot Put

VIII. Techniques of Cross-country Officiating

Suggested officials for a cross-country meet are the same for both men and women. The number of officials necessary to conduct a meet varies. Dual meets will not require as many officials as larger meets. Following is a list of suggested officials, and their duties.

Meet director	1 doctor
1 referee	3 timers
1 starter	1 surveyor
4 finish judges	4-6 inspectors
1 clerk of course	2-4 chute inspectors
1 marshal	running time caller
1 scorer	finish place recorders
1 announcer	time recorder
	trainer

1. Meet Director
   a. shall be directly responsible for the course itself and for securing the officials necessary for the running of the meet.
   b. shall obtain the awards.
   c. shall send out the entry blanks and be their recipient when they are returned.
   d. shall rule upon all late entries or substitutions.
   e. shall procure all equipment necessary for the running of the meet.
   f. shall give the surveyor the specifications for the marking of the course.
   g. shall obtain the completed results and records of the meet from the scorer.

2. Referee
   a. shall confer with other officials prior to the meet to be sure that each has sufficient personnel.
   b. shall ensure (in cooperation with the appointed marshal) that only authorized persons are allowed in the immediate area.
   c. shall see that all rules are observed and decides any technical points which arise during the meet. If there are no set rules covering a dispute, the track referee shall have the final judgment in the matter.
   d. shall have the power to exclude any competitor or official for improper conduct or apparel, and decide immediately any protest or objection about the conduct of a competitor or official.
   e. shall inspect, approve, and sign the scorer's records after the meet.

3. **Starter**
    a. shall be responsible for starting the race in such a manner that all participants start equally. (The official responsibilities of the starter commence after the clerk of course has lined up the participants and instructed them to take off their warmup suits.)
    b. shall be stationed in the middle and 50 yards in front of the starting line.
    c. shall give the first command, a whistle, indicating that all runners must come to the line.
    d. shall give the second vocal command, "runners set" accompanied by raising both arms above the head.
    e. the starter will fire the gun (when all runners are completely motionless).
    f. shall fire a second shot indicating a "false start" (if any runner gains an unfair advantage).

4. **Finish Judges (4)**
    a. shall be stationed at the finish line and decide the finish order of all runners finishing the race.
    b. shall place them in the correct order in the chute or chutes when necessary for large meets.
    c. shall determine who reached the finish line first (if an apparent tie occurs).

5. **Clerk of the Course**
    a. shall be responsible for informing the athletes how much time remains before the race begins.
    b. shall announce when there are 20, 15, 10, and 5 minutes before the race begins. With 5 minutes remaining, the clerk will call all runners to the starting line and line them up in the correct position.
    c. shall warn the runners to stay on course.

6. **Marshal**
    shall police the area and make sure that unauthorized persons do not interfere with judges and timers.

7. **Scorer**
    a. shall record the final race results and also determine the team scores and positions.
    b. shall compile the final result sheet which will include the position, name of school and time of each runner. In addition, it should include the name of the meet, the location, the date, the

distance of the race and weather conditions. Also, if possible, the half mile split times ($\frac{1}{2}$, 1, 1$\frac{1}{2}$, and 2) of the leading runners should be included.

c. shall total the team score which should include the position, the top five runners' finishers, the pushers' (6th and 7th runners) finishers, and the total points for each team. Ties between teams shall be resolved in favor of the team whose last scoring member (the 5th place competitor) finishes nearer the first place. In such cases where the 5th place runners of the tied teams may have tied, the relative positions of the 4th place competitors will determine the winner. *Note:* In larger invitational meets it can be helpful to use a "quick score" system. Here each team runner receives a place card in the finish chute, with the finish position printed on it. Each coach collects these finish cards and places them in an envelope. The team total for the top five members is written on the outside of the envelope and the envelope is turned into a designated "quick score" scorer.

8. Announcer

shall keep the public informed of the progress of the meet. This may be done through the use of walkie-talkies.

9. Timers (3)

a. The timers shall be responsible for all phases of the race and its results that require accurate timing.

b. The Head Timer shall be responsible for coordinating all the timers and timing the first place runner.

c. The second timer will also time first place with the official time being an average of the two times.

d. A timer shall be stationed along the running course at each half mile mark reading the running time to the runners as they pass.

e. A timer shall be stationed at the finish line who will read the final time of each runner as the runner reaches the line. At least 2 running watches shall be kept at the finish line to guard against a single watch malfunction to ensure accurate times for all.

10. Surveyor

clearly marks the course according to the official specifications furnished by the Meet Director.

11. Course Inspectors (4-6)

a. shall be located around the running course at every point where confusion may result and have the responsibility of detecting and reporting in writing all apparent violations of the rules to the referee.

b. the violations are reported first to the chief inspector and then to the referee.

12. Chute Inspectors (2-4)

a. shall supervise the runners after they enter the chute and see that they are properly checked to prevent any irregularity in the order of finish.

b. shall see that any runner who crosses the finish line is given the proper order as the contestants go through the chute.

c. shall instruct contestants in the chute to place a hand on the shoulder of the one in front of them, to prevent gaps in the line.

d. shall designate a substitute for a competitor unable to exit the chute.

13. Finish Place Recorder

a. shall be stationed at the end of the chute and collect each runner's card.

b. shall write the finish position on each card and after collecting the last runner's card, give all the cards to the head scorer.

c. the cards shall have the name and the school of the runner printed on them before the race. This saves time and simplifies the officials' responsibilities.

Note: In large meets a recorder should be assigned to each chute.

14. Time Recorder

a. shall be stationed behind or next to the timer.

b. shall mark down the time of each runner as called out by the timer and give time sheet(s) to the scorer.

15. Athletic Trainer

a. shall provide a first aid training area off the running course near the finish line.

b. shall provide necessary medical supplies and treatment to handle ordinary situations.

c. shall provide both supplies and treatment to visiting teams.

d. shall be available to athletes one hour before the start.

e. shall have immediate transportation and access to a hospital for athletes requiring medical attention.

16. Physician

shall be present in case of serious injuries.

IX. Combined Events Techniques of Officiating

The following officials are necessary to run an efficient combined events meet. All techniques are the same as those followed by NAGWS-ABO officials.

Officials

a. Meet Director—responsible for organizing and running meet.

b. Games Committee—helps meet director in preparation for meet; serves as protest committee.

c. Referee—makes final officiating decisions during meet.

d. Clerk of Course—lines up competitors and gives information prior to races.

e. Starter and Recall Starter—gives information and demonstration of start prior to races; starts races; disqualifies competitor after 3 false starts.

f. Head Timer and Timers—3 per maximum number in any one flight in a running event.

g. Head Inspector and Inspectors—checks equipment and facilities prior to events; watches for violations of rules during running events; reports violations to referee.

h. Head Shot Put Judge and minimum of 3 assistants.

i. Head High Jump Judge and minimum of 2 assistants.

j. Head Long Jump Judge and minimum of 3 assistants.

k. Chief Scorer and assistant (aids and checks scoring).

l. Announcer, assistants at site of events, runner (between announcer and event).

m. Wind Gauge Operator (outdoor).

n. Marshals—spectator control, only athletes should be at site of events.

o. Meet physician and trainers.

p. Hurdle and block setters.

q. Surveyor—surveys facilities prior to meet.

The following comments regarding officiating are also to be expedited.

1. At least ½ hour rest shall be allowed each competitor between consecutive events.

2. In running events and hurdles each competitor shall be timed with three (3) watches. The most frequent or middle time is the official time. If fully automatic timing is used, time and score to the next longer 1/100 second. (Electronic stop watches do not qualify as fully automatic timing.) Hand timing shall be recorded to the next longer 1/10 second.

If the second hand of the watch stops between two lines, the nearest slowest 1/100 or 1/10 shall be accepted. When converting from 1/100 to 1/10 of a second for hand timing, round it to the next longer 1/10 of a second (i.e. 12.44 becomes 12.5). One system of time shall be used throughout the competition.

3. To expedite running the high jump in national competition, it is suggested the bar be raised a minimum of 2 inches (5cm) at a time. The bar should be started at the lowest height requested by an athlete.

4. An athlete disqualified for fouling another competitor in any event shall be permitted to compete in the remaining events, unless the referee shall rule that such a foul was intentional and that mere loss of points is not a sufficient penalty.

5. Where feasible a combined events coordinator should be appointed to see that the events proceed expeditously.

QUESTIONS ON TECHNIQUES

Questions concerning officiating techniques in Track and Field should be directed to:

LURLINE J. JONES
940 E. McPherson St.
Philadelphia, PA 19150

Include a self-addressed, stamped envelope.

TIPS ON
TRAINING

The National Association for Girls and Women in Sport has released its newest publication; <u>Tips on Training.</u>

Coordinated by the NAGWS Athletic Training Council, <u>Tips on Training</u> is designed to serve as both a refresher course for the coach and a source of new information for the seasoned trainer.

A complete source of information, <u>Tips on Training</u> covers the basics of training room organization, injury prevention and emergency care. Also addressed are the new scopes of athletic training and sports medicine research such as the female athlete, the growing athlete and the legal liability of coaches, trainers and educational institutions.

For order and price information call or write: AAHPERD Publication Sales, 1900 Association Dr., Reston, Va. 22091
(703) 476-3481

National Association for
Girls and Women in Sport

Administration of Gymnastics Meets

The National Association for Girls and Women in Sport is pleased to announce the release of its newest publication *Administration of Gymnastics Meets: A Handbook for Coaches and Teachers.*

This handbook, as a 'how-to' for coaches and physical educators will prove to be valuable reading for anyone involved in the administration of gymnastics programs. The reader will be taken through the step by step process of the preliminary and behind the scenes work of a successful gymnastics competition.

For order and price information call or write: AAHPERD Publication Sales, 1900 Association Dr., Reston, Va. 22091 (703) 476-3481

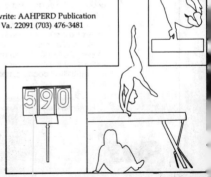

A HANDBOOK
FOR TEACHERS
AND COACHES